# INTRODUCING EGYPTI

*for*
**JUAN, JUANA and PAUL**

# INTRODUCING
# EGYPTIAN HIEROGLYPHS

BY

BARBARA WATTERSON

## SCOTTISH ACADEMIC PRESS
### EDINBURGH

Published by
Scottish Academic Press Ltd,
56 Hanover Street, Edinburgh EH2 2DX

ISBN 0 7073 0738 4

**British Library Cataloguing in Publication Data**

A catalogue record for this book is available
from the British Library

Typeset by Trinity Typesetting
Printed in Great Britain by Antony Rowe Ltd., Chippenham, Wiltshire

# CONTENTS

# ABBREVIATIONS

| | |
|---|---|
| adj. | adjective |
| adv. | adverb |
| cf. | *confer* = compare |
| dep. pron. | dependent pronoun |
| det. | determinative(s) |
| e.g. | *exempli gratia* = for instance |
| f. | feminine |
| ideo. | ideogram |
| lit. | literally |
| m. | masculine |
| phon. | phonetically |
| prep. | preposition |
| sing. | singular |
| var., varr. | variant (s) |

# OUTLINE OF EGYPTIAN CHRONOLOGY

| Dates B.C. (approx.) | Periods | Dynasties | Principal kings |
|---|---|---|---|
| c. 7000-5000 | Palaeolithic | — | — |
| c. 5000-3100 | Neolithic | Predynastic cultures<br>Upper Egypt: Badarian<br>Naqada I & II<br>Lower Egypt: Fayum<br>Merimde | — |
| c. 3100-2890 | Archaic | I | Menes/Narmer |
| c. 2890-2686 | | II | |
| c. 2686-2613 | | III | Zoser |
| c. 2613-2494 | Old Kingdom | IV | Sneferu, Cheops, Chephren, Mycerinus |
| c. 2494-2345 | | V | Sahure, Niuserre, Unas |
| c. 2345-2181 | | VI | Teti, Pepi |
| c. 2181-2160 | First | VII, VIII | Memphite kings |
| c. 2160-2040 | Intermediate | IX, X | Herakleopolitan kings |
| 2134-1991 | Middle | XI | Theban kings |
| 1991-1786 | Kingdom | XII | (from 2040 ruled over whole of Egypt) |

| Dates B.C. (approx.) | Periods | Dynasties | Principal kings |
|---|---|---|---|
| 1786-1551 | Second Intermediate | XIII, XIV XV, XVI, XVII | Hyksos kings |
| 1551-1310 | New Kingdom | XVIII | Amenophis, Tuthmosis, Hatshepsut, Akhenaten, Tutankhamun |
| 1310-1198 | | XIX | Seti, Ramessess II |
| 1198-1087 | | XX | Ramessess III-XI |
| 1087-945 | Third Intermediate | XXI | Psussenes in Tanis Priest-kings in Thebes |
| 945-715 | | XXII | Sheshonq in Bubastis |
| 819-720 | | XXII | Libyan kings in Tanis |
| 728-715 | | XXIV | Saite kings |
| 716-664 | | XXV | Ethiopian kings (Taharqa) |
| 664-525 | | XXVI | Saite kings (Psammeticus) |
| 525-404 | Late Period | XXVI | Persian domination (Cambyses, Darius, Xerxes) |
| 404-378 | | XXVIII, XXIV | Last native kings |
| 378-341 | | XXX | |
| 341-332 | | XXXI | Persian domination (Darius III) |

| Dates B.C. to A.D. | Periods | Dynasties | Ruling Bodies & Kings |
|---|---|---|---|
| 332-30 | Ptolemaic | XXXII | Alexander the Great, Ptolemy, Cleopatra |
| 30 B.C.-A.D. 284 | Roman | — | |
| 284-640 | Byzantine | — | (*Christian Egypt*) |
| 640 | *Arab conquest* | | (*Muslim Egypt*) |
| 868 | | Tulunid | Ibn Tulun |
| 969 | | Fatimid | |
| 1171 | Syrian | Ayyubid | Saladin |
| 1250-1517 | Turkish | Mameluke | |
| 1516-1798 | Ottoman | | Pashas appointed by Turkish Sultan |
| 1798 | | | Napoleon |
| 1801-1882 | Turkish | | Mehemet Ali (1801-1848) |
| 1882-1919 | British protectorate | | |
| 1919-1952 | Independent but bound to Britain by Treaty | | Farouk (1935-1952) |
| 1952-present | Independent Republic | | Gamel Abdel Nasser, Anwar Sadat, presidents |

# PART I

General introduction and background
to hieroglyphic writing in Egypt
and to the principles of picture writing

# INTRODUCING EGYPTIAN HIEROGLYPHS

## INTRODUCTION

In prehistoric times, possibly from about 6000 BC, the population of Egypt was divided into tribal groups. Gradually, the tribes living in settlements on the banks of the Nile in the north of the country and the Delta came together to form the "kingdom" of Lower Egypt, whilst the tribes who lived in the south of Egypt united to form the "kingdom" of Upper Egypt. Shortly before 3100 BC two important events took place. One was the introduction of writing into Egypt (see page 34) which, by definition, marked the transition of Egypt from a prehistoric culture with no written language, and marked the beginning of Egyptian history. The other was the conquest of Lower Egypt by an Upper Egyptian king named Narmer, who thus united the two halves of Egypt (known to the Egyptians as the Two Lands) under a single ruler, himself. The Unification of Egypt was followed by three thousand years of history which is known today as the dynastic period, so called because of the division into dynasties of the kings who ruled Egypt during that time. This system was first introduced by the scholar-priest, Manetho, who lived in the third-century BC, probably at Sebennytos in the Nile Delta. The original system of Manetho consisted of thirty dynasties; it was later enlarged to include those kings who reigned after Manetho's death. A chronology of Egypt, based on Manetho's system, is given on pages ix-xi.

The most notable feature of the dynastic period of the civilization of ancient Egypt was its buildings. Not houses, or even palaces, but temples and tombs. Every Egyptian, from the king down to the poorest peasant, lived in a house built largely of mud-brick and wattle and daub - all perishable materials. The gods, and the dead, were housed in monuments made of stone, designed, the Egyptians thought, to endure for eternity. The passage of time, however, saw the disappearance of many Egyptian monumental buildings together with their contents. The Egyptians buried valuable grave goods with their dead: human nature being what it is, the practice of tomb robbery is almost as old as the tombs themselves. The kings of Egypt were eager to build temples for their gods and tombs for themselves: they often found it expedient to use the material from a predecessor's buildings instead of quarrying for their own. Thus the depredations of men inflicted even more damage than those of Nature.

Of course, ancient Egypt was ancient even to the ancient Egyptians! A man born in Dynasty XX, around 1100 BC, would have considered the Great Pyramid at Giza, one of the Seven Wonders of the Ancient World, built in Dynasty IV, very ancient - in Dynasty XX it was some 1,550 years old. The Great Pyramid was almost as remote in time from him as the Roman invasion of Britain in 55 BC is from us. If we consider that King Arthur, one of the legendary heroes of Britain, was probably a chieftain in late-Roman Britain who, if he existed at all, lived 1,550 years ago, we should not be surprised if the Egyptian of Dynasty XX knew as little of conditions in Egypt during Dynasty IV as we know of King Arthur and his times.

And so, throughout Egyptian history, time and human nature took their toll of Egypt's monuments. From the seventh century BC, Egypt suffered from foreign invaders who, in their turn, inflicted yet more damage - Assyrians, Persians, Greeks and Romans all contributed to the disappearance of ancient Egypt. The Romans, especially, were collectors of everything Egyptian, and great numbers of antiquities, from statues, large and small, to obelisks, those giant shafts of granite which can be hundreds of tons in weight, were shipped back to Rome.

When Egypt was converted to Christianity, the destruction went on. The Egyptians abandoned their old pagan temples and allowed the sand which is ever-present in Egypt to engulf large areas of them. Parts of some temples were turned into churches. Temples, and even tombs, were used as dwelling places. Where tomb and temple reliefs were not damaged deliberately because of religious fervour, or because of superstition and fear of the "evil eye", they were damaged by dirt and misuse, and blackened by cooking fires. Christian Egyptians were followed from the seventh century AD onwards by Muslim Egyptians with the same attitudes towards their ancient pagan monuments. For many centuries, the *fellahin* (peasants) of Egypt have known that the soil from archaeological sites, which is rich in nitrates, makes good *sebakh,* or fertiliser, and even today take whatever opportunities they can to dig for it, thus disturbing the site and often damaging what lies under the sandy soil.

The perennial enemy of all buildings in Egypt, ancient or modern, is sand. A constant battle has always had to be fought to keep them clear of it. Once Egypt had ceased to exist as a great civilization (in 30 BC, with the defeat of Antony and Cleopatra by Octavianus Caesar which resulted in the country becoming a province of Rome) the struggle to keep tombs, temples and other monumental buildings free of sand was largely abandoned. Much of what remained of Egypt's past was lost beneath the sand for centuries. The sand, however, aided by the country's warm, dry climate, kept what was beneath it in a relatively good state of preservation; and hid it from sight, thus saving much of Egypt's archaeological heritage from destruction at the hands of those who were ignorant of what they were doing. Until, in the nineteenth century AD, scholars arrived in Egypt who were interested enough in its past to want to clear away the sand, to study what it had covered and preserved for centuries, and to value what they found.

# Chapter 1

## NAPOLEON'S EXPEDITION TO EGYPT

On 16th August 1797, Napoleon Bonaparte wrote: "In order to destroy England utterly, we must get possession of Egypt" — and thus gain a springboard from which to attack the jewel in Britain's crown, India. Less than a year later, as the newly-appointed "Commander of the army against England", he put his plan into action. As he told his secretary, Bourrienne, an invasion of England would be "too chancy", and so he proposed instead to invade Egypt. On 5th March 1798, the Directors of the French Republic empowered Napoleon to raise the army and fleet necessary to mount an expedition to Egypt.

Egypt had been a province of the Ottoman Empire since 1517 and was governed by a ruling class, the Mamelukes, who were descendants of Caucasian slave-troops originally brought to Egypt by the Turks in 1250. The first aim of Napoleon's Expedition to Egypt was to free the country from the Turks and Mamelukes and bring it under the aegis of France. Only then would Egypt become a secure base from which to launch an attack on Britain's prize possession, India. A second, and from an Egyptological point of view the most important, aim was an entirely original one for which Napoleon himself must be given credit. He proposed to go to Egypt not only to "improve the lot of the natives of Egypt" but, by instituting a programme of mapping, exploration, observation and recording, to open up a country which was almost unknown to Europeans.

Thus, in the interests of scientific discovery, Napoleon began to recruit an army of artists, scientists and scholars. In less than three months, he had assembled 150 "learned civilians", amongst whom were Geoffroy Saint-Hilaire, naturalist; Gratet de Dolomien, mineralogist, after whom the Dolomites were named; Dominique-Vivant Denon, draughtman and engraver; Claude Bertholet, chemist; Dominique Larrey, surgeon; Guillaume Villoteau, musician; Marie-Jules de Savigny, botanist; Pierre Redouté, flower-painter; and Nicolas Conté, the inventor of the lead pencil.

On 19th May 1798, Napoleon sailed from Toulon with 17,000 troops on board an armada of 180 ships. This fleet was supplemented by more than 200 ships sailing from Italian ports, enabling Napoleon to arrive in Egypt with an army of 55,000 men. They arrived at Marabout beach on the north coast of Egypt on 2nd July. Within hours, Napoleon had marched the 13 km to Alexandria and had occupied the city for the loss of 200 men wounded. A French garrison was set up in Alexandria and then the army set out for Cairo, some 200 km to the south east. For two weeks the French struggled through the desert, during the hottest season, plagued by dysentery, black flies and scorpions. On 21st July they emerged from their ordeal to find the Egyptian army drawn up before them in the shadow of the Pyramids at Giza. This army consisted of 16,000 soldiers spear-headed by an élite cavalry of 8,000 Mamelukes under the command of the ruler of Egypt, the Circassian, Murad Bey.

Napoleon had virtually no cavalry of his own; he did, however, have infantry and artilliary. On the morning of the battle he made a speech to his troops. Pointing to the three pyramids towering above them he began, "Soldiers, from the height of these pyramids, forty centuries look down upon you!" The ensuing Battle of the Pyramids was a rout. Although the Mamelukes were crack soldiers and horsemen whose lives were dedicated to fighting, they could not hope to overcome the French rifles and bayonets. The Egyptian infantry, which had never before faced heavy guns, panicked and fled. In less than two hours Napoleon had destroyed or captured most of the Egyptian army together with the Mameluke cavalry. Murad Bey escaped with only a handful of men.

On 25th July Napoleon entered Cairo and declared Turkish rule at an end. However, his satisfaction was to be short-lived. On 7th August the Battle of the Nile was fought in Aboukir Bay. The British fleet under the command of Admiral Lord Nelson destroyed thirteen out of the seventeen French warships and mounted a blockade of Egypt. Napoleon and his 55,000 men were cut off, unable to receive supplies and reinforcements from France. On the morning when he received the news from Aboukir Bay,

Napoleon is said to have gone into breakfast with his officiers observing, "It seems you like this country. That is very lucky, for we now have no fleet to carry us back to Europe."

Napoleon's Egyptian Expedition lasted for another year. In July 1799 he received news from Europe, the first he had had in six months, which gave him cause for considerable alarm. France now had not only Britain for an enemy, but Austria, Russia, Naples and Turkey also. She was on the verge of economic collapse; and there was talk of restoring the monarchy. Napoleon decided that his only course was to run the British blockade and make his way back to France, to "the spot where (he) could be of most use." Accordingly, on 23rd August 1799, he left his army in Egypt and sailed for France.

The fourteen months that Napoleon spent in Egypt set in motion the scientific examination of its antiquities which laid the foundations of modern Egyptology. In August 1798 Napoleon founded a learned academy in Cairo based on the Institut de France in Paris to coordinate the researches of the 150 "learned civilians" who had accompanied his army to Egypt. He made the mathematician, Gaspard Monge, president, and he himself became the vice-president. The Cairo Institute met every five days, and Napoleon spent so much time there that his officers became jealous and spoke contemptuously of the scholars, calling them "Pekinese dogs", inferring that they were merely Napoleon's lap-dogs. Napoleon was already a member of the Paris Institut's mathematical section and his Egyptian studies, therefore, had a mathematical bent.

The "Pekinese dogs" undertook a variety of projects. Berthollet studied the natron (sodium carbonate) lakes in the Western Desert and the manufacture of indigo. Villoteau studied Arab music, Larrey ophthalmia. Savigny discovered a new species of water-lily. Saint-Hilaire made detailed studies of ostriches and crocodiles, and of the polypterus, a species of fish peculiar to tropical Africa. Through his study of mummified ibises, Saint-Hilaire became the first man to follow the development of a species through several thousand years. By means of his work on comparative anatomy he paved the way for Charles Darwin.

It was the work of the Academician, Dominique-Vivant Denon, which had the most far-reaching effects on the study of ancient Egypt. Denon was fifty years old and had led an eventful life. During a career as a diplomat, his posts had ranged from secretary at the French Embassy in St Petersburg, where he was reputed to be a lover of Catherine the Great, to an assignment in Switzerland where he was often a guest of Voltaire and where he had painted the famous *Breakfast at Ferney.* During the French Revolution, Denon had lived in penury in the slums of Paris on such money as he could raise by selling his drawings. Eventually, he came to the attention of Jacques Louis David, the great Revolutionary painter, who gave him work as his engraver thus enabling Denon to be rehabilitated. Denon had then achieved some success as an author, writing a classic short love story, *Le point de lendemain;* and an even greater success when he produced the *Oeuvre priapique*, a collection of pornographic etchings.

Before the Revolution, Denon had been a favourite of Madame de Pompadour; after it he became a protégé of Josephine Beauharnais, who recommended him to Napoleon for the Egyptian Expedition. Denon had come to Egypt as a draughtsman; and it was his talent for drawing that enabled him to play a vital role in the history of Egyptology. From the moment he set foot in Egypt, Denon fell in love with all things Egyptian. When General Desaix set off for Upper Egypt in pursuit of the defeated Mameluke leader Murad Bey, Denon went with him. Desaix chased Murad Bey as far as Aswan, some 1000 km south of Cairo, and defeated and killed him at the battle of Sediman. All the time, Denon sketched away, "mostly on my knee or standing, even on horseback, and without finishing even one as I should have liked."

Denon made hundreds of sketches of the antiquities of ancient Egypt, from the Step Pyramid at Sakkara to the tombs and temples of Thebes (Luxor); from the temples of Dendera and Edfu to the chapel of Amenhotep III at Aswan. Denon's drawing of this chapel is the only one extant: the building itself was pulled down in 1822. As he worked, Denon could not fail to notice that many of the monuments he was sketching were covered with inscriptions, strange, beautiful, pictorial writings — hieroglyphs. Nobody with Desaix's army could tell him what these hieroglyphs were, or what they meant. Nevertheless, he took pains to copy as accurately as possible what he saw.

Meantime, other members of Napoleon's group of "learned civilians" were busy copying inscriptions from Egyptian monuments; so much so that they ran out of pencils and Conté had to improvise new ones by melting down lead bullets into holders made from reeds which grew along the banks of the Nile. The "learned civilians" did not understand the hieroglyphic signs any better than Denon: however, they consulted ancient Greek writers and decided, erroneously, that the Greeks had been correct in their belief that ancient Egyptian was basically the same language as Chinese.

By chance, the key to unlocking the secret of Egyptian hieroglyphs was discovered by an insignificant French soldier named d'Hautpoul. In August 1799 a gang of men, under the direction of an engineer-officer named Bouchard, were working in the ruins of Fort Rashid near Rosetta, a coastal town some 70 km east of Alexandria. D'Hautpoul dug up a piece of black basalt just over a metre long and nearly a metre wide, one side of which was covered with columns of inscriptions. There was a damaged section containing fourteen lines of the usual mysterious hieroglyphs; thirty-two lines of an even stranger form of writing (later found to be demotic — see page 39); and fifty-four lines of Greek. Luckily, the importance of the Rosetta Stone, as d'Hautpoul's piece of basalt came to be known, was recognised immediately; and Bouchard had it taken to Cairo for further study.

In July 1799 the most important session of the Cairo Institute was held. The savant, Lancret, announced "the discovery at Rosetta of some inscriptions that may offer much interest." Lancret, who had read the Greek inscription on the Rosetta Stone, was able to reveal that it was a decree issued by the priests of Memphis to commemorate the coronation of Ptolemy V, Epiphanes, in 196 BC. It was reasonable to suppose that the inscriptions written in the other two scripts contained the same text; and it was understood that these scripts were both ancient Egyptian, with one, the hieroglyphic, being the formal script; and the other, the demotic, being the cursive script "of the people" or "of the country", which is what the word demotic means. It was considered that the hieroglyphic script was perhaps more accurate than the demotic; and that by comparing the Greek text with the hieroglyphic version it should be possible to arrive at a decipherment of the hieroglyphs.

Plaster copies of the Rosetta Stone were sent to Paris. Soon, scholars in Germany, Italy, England and France were at work on the task of deciphering the hieroglyphs. All to no avail. Every scholar started from false premises, based on ideas propounded by ancient Greek writers who thought that each hieroglyph had a symbolic meaning. Finally, Silvestre de Sacy, perhaps the greatest expert of his day in oriental languages, announced that hieroglyphs remained "untouched as the Holy Ark of the Covenant". Furthermore, "the problem is too complicated, scientifically insoluble."

France's hold on Egypt did not long survive the departure of Napoleon and by 1801 the French had been defeated by both the Turks and the British. The remnants of Napoleon's expeditionary force to Egypt were repatriated, although most of the "learned civilians" stayed behind in Egypt and continued their work as best they could until they, too, were finally returned to France. Many of the Egyptian antiquities that had been collected by the French, including the Rosetta Stone, were handed over to the British; and General Hutchinson arranged for their transportation to England where George III instructed that they be housed in the British Museum.

By 1804 Egypt was under the rule of a man who had been sent there by the Turkish Government to fight the French - Mehemet Ali, who had been born in Kavala in Macedonia and who had risen through the ranks of the Turkish Army to be commander of Albanian troops. Mehemet Ali, better-known as Mohammed Ali, retained the link with France, thus enabling French scientists and academics to influence the development of Egyptian scholarship. He also began to modernize the country, one of the results of which was the opening up of Egypt to Egyptologists. Mohammed Ali knew nothing about ancient Egypt, and cared less, but if it amused foreigners to come to Egypt and study the monuments, he was willing to allow it for the sake of good relations with foreign governments.

By 1806 Napoleon's "Pekinese dogs" were much reduced in number. Of the original band of scholars who had accompanied Napoleon to Egypt, five had been killed in battle, five assassinated, one had been drowned, ten had died of plague and five of dysentery, and five had died in France from the effects of their sojourn in Egypt. Many had impaired health, their eyesight being especially badly affected due to sun, sand

and dust, not to mention the flies which spread the eye diseases which were endemic amongst the Egyptian populace.

Those who remained, however, set to work to publish the discoveries they had made in Egypt. In 1802, Vivant Denon published his *Journey in Upper and Lower Egypt;* and between 1809 and 1813 François Jomard published his great work, *Descriptions of Egypt,* which was based on the work of the Institute which Napoleon had founded in Cairo and made full use of Denon's superb drawings. Thus scholars everywhere gained access to all the discoveries made to date in Egypt. Laymen had a new world opened up to them, a world that they had never before glimpsed and which was unlike anything they had ever known. Public interest in the fascinating science of Egyptology had begun.

One major mystery remained. If the history of ancient Egypt were ever to be known, if Egypt were ever to be seen through the eyes of the ancient Egyptians themselves, then the secret of hieroglyphs must be unravelled.

**Chapter II**

**THE DECIPHERMENT OF HIEROGLYPHS**

The earliest hieroglyphic inscriptions in Egypt go back to at least 3100 BC. The script in which they were written lived on into the Christian era, and the latest-known hieroglyphic inscription, dated to 24th August AD 394, in the reign of the Byzantine Emperor Theodosius, is to be found on the island of Philae, south of Aswan. By the fifth century AD the understanding of hieroglyphs had been lost altogether.

When Alexander the Great conquered Egypt in 332 BC, hieroglyphs had for some time been used almost exclusively for inscriptions carved on temple walls or public monuments. They were understood by a rapidly diminishing number of people, mostly priests: hence the Macedonian Greeks who ruled Egypt after Alexander called them "sacred" (Greek: *hieros*) "sculptures" (Greek: *glupho*), from which is derived the term "hieroglyphs".

Greek and Roman writers such as Herodotus, Strabo and Diodorus Siculus, who visited Egypt, all referred to hieroglyphs as a form of picture writing which was completely unintelli-gible. In the fourth century AD, Horapollo, who was perhaps a Hellenised Egyptian, made a survey of Egyptian writing, and published a list of nearly 200 hieroglyphs together with his interpretation of their meaning, in his *Hieroglyphica*. He established a tradition which was followed by later writers, notably those of the Renaissance onwards who had access to a manuscript of Horapollo's work found early in the fifteenth century. They all looked for a symbolic meaning for each hieroglyphic sign, expecting a picture of three wavy lines to mean water, and only water; similarly, a picture of a head to mean a head, that of an owl to mean an owl, and so on. They made no allowance for the fact that such pictures may, in fact, be phonograms (signs which denote sounds), or, indeed, letters of an alphabet rather than simply pictographs.

The symbolic interpretation of hieroglyphs was further elaborated by the theory that they had an allegorical meaning founded on traditional Egyptian stories and philosophies. This belief led to some very fanciful translations. Horapollo, for example, pointed out that the picture of a vulture stood for the word "mother". This is correct: the ancient Egyptian word for mother is *mwt* (pronounced "moot") and is, in this case, represented by a *phonogram*. That is, the word for vulture is the same as that meaning mother; hence the picture of a vulture is used to denote "mother" because both words have the *same sound*. Horapollo, however, did not recognise this fact: his explanation was that the picture of a vulture was in this instance used in a metaphorical way to represent the idea of motherhood because, he believed, female vultures were able to reproduce without the aid of males — motherhood *par excellence*!

The purely ideographic and symbolic interpretation of hieroglyphic writing prevented any true decipherment being made. It did not, however, prevent many ingenious, but completely erroneous, versions of hieroglyphic texts being produced with confidence. The most famous of these interpretations was published between 1652 and 1654 by the Jesuit, Athanasius Kircher, in his *Oedipus Aegyptiacus*. Kircher was a professor of mathematics in the University of Rome whose interests were many and varied. He was adept at music, geology and astronomy, and was a competent philologist. He took a special interest in the language that was used in the liturgy of the Christian Church in Egypt, Coptic.

Having made a study of Coptic manuscripts brought back to Europe by an Italian nobleman named Pietro della Valle, Kircher compiled the first Coptic grammar to be published in Europe. His great contribution to the decipherment of hieroglyphs lies in his recognition that the Coptic language was the direct descendant of the language of Egypt spoken in Pharaonic times. Working back from the Coptic is still an important aid to the study of the earlier stages of the native language of Egypt. Kircher, however, was interested in the script in which the language of ancient Egypt had been written — hieroglyphic. He professed to have found the key to its decipherment. The translations which he published in *Oedipus Aegyptiacus* were based on the by then traditional theory that all Egyptian hieroglyphs had a symbolic meaning. Although Kircher genuinely believed that his understanding of Egyptian philosophy was so perfect that it enabled him to produce a viable translation, his interpretations of the texts, ingenious as they were, were nonsense.

It might be expected that the discovery of the Rosetta Stone in 1799 would have put an end to speculation about the correct way in which to read hieroglyphs. This was not so. The Stone sparked off a spate of attempts to decipher hieroglyphs, but most of them were as fanciful as all such attempts in the past had been. Many interpretations were placed on them, from quotations from the Bible, to astrological and religious doctrines, to excerpts from Chaldean, Hebrew and even Chinese literature. J-F. Champollion (see below) realised the absurdity of such ideas and remarked, "It was as if the Egyptians had nothing to express in their own language."

Three men, one French, the others Scandinavian, must be given the credit for putting scholars onto the right lines regarding the decipherment of hieroglyphs. First, the French Sinologist, Charles de Guignes (1721-1800), who recognised that some groups of hieroglyphic signs had determinatives, that is, signs which determine the meaning of the foregoing hieroglyphs. Second, Georg Zoëga (1755-1809), the Danish antiquarian who arrived at the conclusion that many hieroglyphs represented letters of an alphabet. Zoëga also put forward an idea that was later to prove vitally important, the idea that the cartouches, that is, the elongated oval shapes, ⟨ ⟩, which are thought to represent loops of rope, and which are found in many inscriptions, contained royal names. We now know that the cartouche (a French word meaning a scroll or tablet designed to take an inscription) was called "shenou" by the Egyptians, and signified everything that was encircled by the sun. The cartouche, therefore, shows that the king whose name is written inside it is monarch of all that the sun surveys. Third, Johan Åkerblad (1763-1819), a Swedish diplomat, who compared the Greek and demotic texts on the Rosetta Stone and identified all the proper names which occur in both texts. He was thus able to publish his version of a demotic alphabet in 1802 in his *Lettre à M. de Sacy*. He got no further with his studies because he mistakenly believed that the demotic system of writing was entirely alphabetic.

The next great step was taken by Thomas Young (1773-1829), the eminent English scientist. In 1814 he obtained a copy of the Rosetta Stone and from this he achieved some outstanding results in deciphering the demotic section of the Stone. He realised that the demotic system of writing was closely connected with the hieroglyphic. Further, he proved that although some demotic signs represented letters of an alphabet others did not. Turning to the Greek section, Young noticed that many words were repeated several times. Working from this basis, he divided the demotic section into its component words. Eventually he was able to form a Greek-Demotic vocabulary of eighty-six groups of words, most of them correct; and went on to study material other than the Rosetta Stone. Sadly, he was hindered in his progress because he was not a philologist and because he did not have sufficient knowledge of the Coptic that was to prove an indispensable aid to the decipherment of hieroglyphs.

The man who finally solved the mystery of hieroglyphs was Jean-François Champollion. He was born nine years before the discovery of the Rosetta Stone, on 23rd December 1790, in the French town of Figeac in the Dauphiné, the son of a bookseller. Jean-François was seven years old when the word Egypt first took on significance for him, thanks to his brother, Jacques-Joseph, then nineteen years old and a gifted philologist, who tried and failed to join Napoleon's Expedition to Egypt. Four years later, in 1801, Jacques-Joseph took his young brother to Grenoble so that he could take charge of his education.

Shortly after his arrival in Grenoble, Jean-François visited the home of Jean-Baptiste Fourier, a mathematician and physicist who had been on the Egyptian Expedition. Fourier showed the younger Champollion his collection of Egyptian antiquities, thus prompting him to enquire whether anyone could read the hieroglyphic inscriptions on them. When told "No" he announced: "I am going to do it. In a few years I will be able to", adding, like any child of his age, "when I am big." From then on, however, his preparations were not childlike; and his studies were all directed towards enabling him to fulfil his promise.

Jean-François had shown a precocious talent for Latin, Greek and Hebrew; and by the time he was thirteen years old he had begun to learn several oriental languages, including Arabic and Coptic. The eclectic Champollion then took up the study of Old

Chinese, Persian and Parsi. Coptic was his great love. He knew that it was an Egyptian language that was written in Greek characters; and that it had been spoken and written in Egypt, especially by Christian Egyptians, from about the third to the sixteenth century AD. In Champollion's day, it was understood by some of the priests of the Coptic Church which was still flourishing in parts of Egypt. Champollion was convinced, correctly, that Coptic was really a late form of that same Egyptian language which was concealed in the hieroglyphs. By the age of sixteen, Champollion spoke and read Coptic so well that he kept journals in it. By 1807 Champollion had prepared an historical chart of ancient Egypt, drawn entirely from Biblical references, Latin, Hebrew and Arabic texts, supplemented by Coptic. The seventeen-year-old Champollion presented his paper *Egypt under the Pharaohs* to the teaching staff of the Lycée at Grenoble, and was immediately made a member of the faculty.

Champollion first saw a copy of the inscriptions on the Rosetta Stone in Fourier's house in Grenoble. In 1808, he obtained a facsimile of the Stone which had been made from the original which was, and is, housed in the British Museum. His initial attempt at decipherment led him to find values for several letters, but his satisfaction at such a good beginning was short-lived as news reached him that hieroglyphs had been deciphered by the Egyptologist and antiquarian, Alexandre Lenoir (1762-1839). However, as soon as Champollion had obtained a copy of Lenoir's *Nouvelle explication des hiéroglyphes* he realised that the theories in this four-volume work were sheer invention.

Champollion continued to work on the Rosetta Stone. It was known already from Zoëga's work that the cartouches on the Stone contained royal names. Åkerblad had identified the name Ptolemaios (Ptolemy in English) in the Greek and demotic sections. Champollion, looking for the name Ptolemaios in the hieroglyphic section, found

on the sixth line.

By assuming that the name in this cartouche was to be read alphabetically, with each hieroglyph representing a separate letter; and by reading the hieroglyphs in the same order as the demotic, that is, from right to left, Champollion arrived at the reading p-t-o-l-m-y-s, which he took to be the approximation in Egyptian to the Greek Ptolemaios (πτολεμαιοϲ). He was thus able to draw up a tentative sign list, matching the hieroglyphs with letters in the Roman alphabet in which his own language, French, was written, as follows:

$$\square \quad = p$$

$$\frown \quad = t$$

= o

= l

= m

= y

= s

By sheer chance, Champollion was to have the opportunity to confirm his theories thanks to Mr William John Bankes, an English Parliamentarian and antique collector who had been aide-de-camp to the Duke of Wellington in the Peninsular War of 1808-14. Bankes travelled extensively in the Near East and visited Egypt and Nubia. In 1815 he discovered two red granite obelisks on the island of Philae, just south of Aswan in Egypt. They had been erected by Ptolemy VIII, Euergetes, and his wives, Kleopatra II and Kleopatra III. One of the obelisks had been badly damaged, only about a third of it remaining. Nevertheless, Bankes arranged for Giovanni Belzoni, the Italian "antiquarian", to ship both obelisks to Britain, where eventually, on 17th August 1827, they were set up in the grounds of Bankes's house, Kingston Lacy,[1] at Wimborne in Dorset, on a spot chosen by the Duke of Wellington.

---

[1]   Now owned by the National Trust and open to the Public.

The plinth of the unbroken Philae obelisk bears an inscription in Greek in which the two Kleopatras and Ptolemy are named. The shaft of the obelisk is inscribed in hieroglyphs; and Bankes, and Thomas Young, whom he consulted, thought that the hieroglyphic inscription was a direct translation of the Greek. They suggested that since there were two names written in cartouches on the shaft of the obelisk, one of which was identical with the name Ptolemy as written on the Rosetta Stone, the other must be the hieroglyphic version of Kleopatra.

Bankes had little time for Champollion, but nevertheless in 1822 Champollion was given a copy of the inscriptions found on the unbroken Philae obelisk and was able to confirm that the obelisk was, in effect, a second Rosetta Stone as far as the royal names were concerned, although the text on the shaft of the obelisk was not the same as that on the plinth. When he examined the hieroglyphic inscriptions on the Philae obelisk he was immediately able to pick out the cartouche bearing the name p-t-o-l-m-y-s (Ptolemaios) which he knew already from the Rosetta Stone. The Greek inscriptions referred also to Kleopatra; and Champollion was able to isolate the relevant cartouche in the hieroglyphs on the shaft:

When Champollion made a comparison of the two royal names on the shaft of the Philae obelisk, he discovered that some of the hieroglyphic characters found in the name Ptolmys looked the same as some of those in the cartouche which he was

*Introducing Egyptian Hieroglyphs*

assuming held the name Kleopatra (cartouche illustrated above):

  p  t  o  l  m  y  s

    l    o  p        t (?)

Assuming that pronunciation would be similar to the Greek, he deduced that ◿ was
k, 🦅 was a, ⊖ was d, ⊂ was r; and that whereas ⁴⁴ was y, ⁴ was i. He had two
different letters for t - a △ from Ptolemaios, and a ⊖ from Kleopatra. He concluded
that they were homophones, that is, equally valid symbols for the same sound (like f and
ph in English).

Young had already observed that the signs △◯ always occurred at the ends of the
names of goddesses and queens. Therefore the △◯ at the end of the name Kleopatra
was simply an ending denoting a female who was considered divine. Champollion was
able to make a transliteration of the cartouche as follows:

  k   l   i   o   p   a   t   r   a

Later it was established that ⊖ is in fact d and that 𝔩 is w, so that the names
Ptolemaios and Kleopatra are more correctly transliterated, that is, turned into an
approximation of the English alphabet, as Ptwlmys and Kliwpadra, which gives an
indication of how the natives of ancient Egypt pronounced these foreign (Macedonian
Greek) names.

Champollion went on to test his phonetic approach on as many cartouches as he could find, limiting the field at this stage to those of the Graeco-Roman period. Within months he had transliterated over eighty, amongst which were those of Alexander, Berenice, Tiberius, Domitian and Trajan. His sign list grew apace: but a doubt remained. Would his system, which worked so well for the Graeco-Roman names, be equally effective when applied to the cartouches of an earlier age? Or did the Egyptians only use hieroglyphs phonetically when dealing with foreign names?

An opportunity to test whether his theories worked with ancient Egyptian names came in September 1822 when Champollion received copies of reliefs from a temple which lay between the First and Second Cataracts of the Nile at Abu Simbel, a temple which has become famous in modern times because of its dramatic rescue in the 1960s from submersion under the water of the reservoir behind the High Dam at Aswan. Two temples had been discovered at Abu Simbel at the beginning of the nineteenth century by the Anglo-Swiss traveller, John Lewis Burckhardt; but it was not until August 1817 that the larger of the two was cleared of the sand that had engulfed it. At that time, the name of the king for whom the temple had been built was not known because, of course, the hieroglyphic inscriptions in the temple could not be read. Examining the cartouches from Abu Simbel, Champollion found one which read:

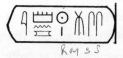

Champollion knew already that ⌐ was the sound s; he had given the value m to the sign 𝕏 (actually, it is ms). The sign ☉ was obviously meant to be the sun; in Coptic, the word for sun is *re*. Putting all this information together, he came up with a reading for the signs in the right-hand side of the cartouche. ☉𝕏⌐⌐ might be made up of a phonogram (that is, a sign representing a sound) ☉ meaning re, and several alphabetic signs, and might, therefore, be read re-m-s-s. The name of the Pharaoh, Ramesses (sometimes spelled Rameses), mentioned in the Bible, flashed across his mind. But what about the signs on the left-hand side of the cartouche, ⟨⟩ ? According to his alphabetic list, ⟨⟩ was i and ⟨⟩ was mn. Therefore, he deduced, ⟨⟩ might represent the name of the god whom the Greeks had called Ammon. As for the sign ⟨⟩: he knew from the Greek that a king was often said to be "beloved of" a god. In Coptic, "to love" is *me* or *mere*; perhaps ⟨⟩ was to be read mr (pronounced "mer") and mean "beloved". The left-hand side of the cartouche would therefore be read mr imn and mean "beloved of Ammon". Thus, the inscriptions inside the cartouche were to be read from right to left, giving the translation "Ramesses beloved of Ammon" (now known to be Ramesses II (1304-1238 BC) for whom Abu Simbel was built; Ammon today is written Amun).

Champollion went on to study another cartouche:

The bird on the left-hand side of this cartouche is an ibis, sacred to the god, Thoth. It is followed by two signs, ⟨⟩ and ⟨⟩, to which Champollion had assigned the values m and s. The name in this cartouche must surely be Thoth-m-s or Thothmes, known from Greek records to have been a Pharaoh (Tuthmosis to the Greeks).

Champollion had made a major breakthrough. The secret of ancient Egyptian writing was that it combined signs representing sounds with signs representing ideas. He felt that he was now able to publish his results and on 29th September 1822, at the age of thirty-two, he read his memorable paper, *Lettre à M. Dacier relative à l'alphabet des hiéroglyphes phonétique,* to the members of the Academy in Paris, and won immortal fame. In his letter to M. Dacier Champollion made no mention of his discoveries concerning the decipherment of the names of Ramesses and Thothmes (Tuthmosis), waiting until 1824 to publish these in his *Précis du système hiéroglyphic.* He also failed to mention any debt he might owe to the work of others, notably Åkerblad and Young.

Champollion at long last made a visit to Egypt in 1828-29, interpreting and deciphering. He died three years later, on 4th March 1832, at the age of only forty-one years: but he had laid the foundations on which work on hieroglyphs was to continue. The Germans Karl Richard Lepsius (1810-84), considered by many to be the greatest Egyptologist of them all, Heinrich Brugsch (1827-94) and Kurt Sethe (1869-1934); the Frenchman Jacques de Rougé (1842-1923); and the Italian Niccolo Rosellini (1800-43) all made invaluable contributions: and the work of decipherment went on.

## Chapter III

## HOW WRITING BEGAN: FROM PICTURE WRITING TO THE ALPHABET

The modern system of writing, that is, the system of breaking down the spoken word into its component parts, consisting of vowels and consonants, and representing each of the sounds thus arrived at by alphabetic signs, is very artificial. To the minds of the earliest human beings it would have been impossible to grasp.

Prehistoric people could comprehend pictures of objects and animals; they could understand that a picture of an animal painted upon a cave wall represented a real animal — a not inconsiderable intellectual achievement. It can be seen from cave paintings at sites such as Lascaux in France and Altamira in Spain that as far back as 25,000 years ago prehistoric peoples used cave paintings in their magic ceremonies. Painting an animal on a cave wall, and transfixing it with painted arrows, might have been an attempt by prehistoric men to gain power over the animal and make it vulnerable when they hunted it: thus the painting of the animal had taken the place of the real animal for magical purposes. It is even possible that some cave paintings were used for instructing young hunters: in these paintings the teacher would indicate with painted arrows and other weapons which parts of an animal's body were most vulnerable. If this was indeed one of the purposes of cave paintings it is one of the earliest methods of communicating information other than by speech.

It is easy to imagine that prehistoric hunters might have scratched simple drawings of fish or animals in wet sand or on rocks as a means of indicating to other hunters where quantities of fish or game were to be found. By doing so they were making use of the simple idea that formed the basis of the earliest-known writing. By means of simplified drawings, known to us as *pictographs,* the inventors of writing wrote down

symbols which represented words in their language. Thus a picture of a fish ⌒⌒⌒
denoted a fish, a picture of a face ☺ denoted a face, and so on. Today, the Chinese
and Japanese still base their written language on a pictographic system. In ancient
China, the drawing ⊙ represented the sun, and ☽ the moon. In modern Chinese, the
ancient symbols have been stylised, with the characters for sun and moon, for example, now reading 日 and 月; but the Chinese still write using word pictures or
***logographs.***

There are a vast number of signs in a pictographic system of writing such as
the Chinese, making written Chinese extremely difficult to learn. Japanese presents
the same problem, and Japanese children today learn to read by first using a
system that allows them to break down the written language into a series of
sound signs. Once they have learned to read in a phonological way, which appears to be relatively easy and is usually mastered by the age of six, they transfer
to the normal logographic script. It is said to take about eight years to learn the
2000 logograms of this script, at the rate of between 80 and 300 characters a
year.

Apart from the sheer numbers of signs that must be learned, a pictographic system
of writing has further obvious limitations. Simple pictographs can serve to represent
concrete objects, but they cannot express actions, or abstract ideas such as the verb
"to think". The problem can be solved by the use of ***ideograms,*** that is, symbols which
stand for several related words or concepts. Ideograms, therefore, are ***sense signs.*** In
order to represent a physical action, for instance, a picture can be drawn of a certain
stage in that action: for example, a picture of a man carrying a basket on his head 🏃
could mean "to carry"; similarly, ⌒⌒ could mean "to fall"; 🐦 could mean "to think".
The basic meaning of the pictograph "sun" can be extended into an ideogram meaning
"day" or "daytime". The pictograph of a mouth can be used to indicate the actions of
the mouth — speaking, kissing etc. The pictograph of a foot can denote the verbs "to

go" or "to stand" as well as the noun foot. The meaning of each ideogram has to be judged according to context.

Picture writing which consists entirely of pictographs and ideograms can be very simple, universally understood no matter what language or alphabet the reader of the sign normally uses. For example, a pictograph showing a man would be read as *homme* in French, *hombre* in Spanish, *uomo* in Italian; but the meaning of the sign would be the same for everyone.

Today, universally understood pictographs have been put to good use in many ways. The picture of a man on the door of a public convenience ensures that no women will enter; there is no need for notices saying "men only" in many different languages to be posted. Written notices saying "Look out for wild animals" or "Look out for cattle" can only be understood by someone who reads English; but international road signs bearing the pictographs or can be understood by everyone. However, international road signs do sometimes illustrate that the use of pictographs is not without its problems. Does the sign mean "It is very windy; umbrellas are liable to be blown inside out" or does it mean "Road works"!

In recent years the use of ideograms has become widespread in so-called "user-friendly" computer systems. Commands are given not by typing in or selecting from a list of words but by selecting from a range of ideograms or "icons". The need for a language to describe the many novel concepts in computing has led to the wholesale adoption of familiar (American) English words on the basis of an association, usually tenuous, of ideas. Today, words such as icon, mouse, chip, scroll, boot, paste, forest, tree, and even widow, have entirely new meanings not only within the world of the computer buff but also in everyday school and office life.

Ideograms and pictographs have serious limitations. The story is told of a king who received a message made up of the pictures of a bird, a mouse, a frog and five arrows. It is to be hoped that he interpreted the signs correctly, for the message meant: "Can you fly like a bird, hide in the ground like a mouse, leap through the marshes like a frog? If not, avoid war with us for we shall defeat you with our arrows." And how is one to decipher the following message:

Here we see a simplified drawing of a man with his hand to his mouth (an ideogram denoting an action of some sort), pointing towards a tent (a pictograph representing a concrete object). Does the picture mean "I am hungry and I'm going into my tent to eat"? Or is the man yawning and, politely covering his mouth with his hand, saying, "I am tired. I am going to my tent to sleep"? Or perhaps he is cupping his mouth with his hand and shouting, "Help! My tent is on fire!" He could even be waggling his fingers in front of his mouth and complaining, "My mother-in-law came into my tent an hour ago and she hasn't stopped talking since."!

The solution to the problem of ambiguity in picture writing lies in the transition of such writing from the *purely pictorial* representation of *concrete objects* to the *artificial representation* of *sounds*. The term **phonogram,** or sound sign, is used to describe this more advanced development in picture writing. Phonograms make use of the principle of rebus or charade: that is, they use pictures of things not to represent the things themselves but to indicate something entirely different which is perhaps not easy to put into pictographs, but which chances to have the same or a similar sound as an easily-pictured thing.

Children today sometimes send each other coded messages using the rebus or "play on words" system. For instance, the English verb "I saw" can be rendered, to an English-speaking person, by the drawing of an eye placed next to a drawing of a saw: . Similarly, a drawing of a bee can be placed next to a drawing of a leaf ; the resulting picture-word, to be pronounced "bee-leaf", is spelled differently yet possesses the same sound as the noun "belief", and can therefore be used to denote that word.

An essential difference between pictographs and phonograms is that whereas pictographs can be universally understood regardless of the language spoken by the writer or reader of the pictograph, phonograms can only be understood by speakers of the language which has been used to make up the "play on words" which has produced the phonogram. A phonogram playing on French words will make no sense to a non-French speaker, just as a phonogram playing on German words will be unintelligible to someone who does not speak German. The same difficulty is apparent with picture writing in general. Whilst it may be clear enough what a pictograph represents, it will tell you nothing about the language of the person who wrote it.

A pictographic system of writing is, of course, not nearly so convenient to use as an *alphabetic* system, that is, a system in which each of a minimum number of signs represents a single simple sound in a language. Today, most western European languages, including English, are written in the *Roman alphabet,* which has twenty-six letters. Since the basic Roman alphabet is not large enough to accommodate all the sounds in these languages, accent marks have had to be added to some letters in order to allow one letter to indicate several different sounds. In French, for example, accented letters include é, è, à, ç; in German, ä and ö. In some languages, extra letters have been added to the original twenty-six-letter Roman alphabet — the German ß (= ss) and the Danish ø, for example. Other languages use a Roman alphabet of less than twenty-six letters: Serbo-Croat has no q,w,x or y; the Hawaiian language uses an alphabet of only twelve letters. Gaelic is written in an alphabet of eighteen letters which is derived from the Roman.

There are several alphabets other than the Roman in common use. The *Greek alphabet*, which has twenty-four letters, is used in Greece and by scientists. The word "alphabet" comes from its first two letters, A (alpha) and B (beta). The *Cyrillic alphabet*, which has thirty-three letters, is used in Russia and other Slavic countries such as Bulgaria. It was adapted from the Greek alphabet in the ninth century AD by St Cyril, a Greek priest who, having been sent to convert the Slavs of Bulgaria and Moravia to

Christianity, wanted to write the Gospels in their language. The *Hebrew alphabet,* which has twenty-two letters and unlike the Roman alphabet is written from right to left, is used in Israel. The *Arabic alphabet,* which has twenty-eight letters and is also written from right to left, is used in Arabic-speaking countries throughout the world; but the spread of Islam from the seventh century AD onwards imposed it on a variety of languages other than Arabic, from Persian, an Aryan language, to Hindustani, another Aryan language spoken in parts of India, to Turkish, a Tatar language.

Some languages use two alphabets. Serbo-Croat is written in the Cyrillic alphabet in Serbia and in the Roman alphabet in Croatia. Occasionally, it is decided to change from one alphabet to another. This happened in Turkey in 1928 when the Turks dropped the use of the Arabic alphabet in favour of the Roman alphabet because their ruler, Kemal Ataturk, considered that this would be an advantage to a country striving to enter the modern European world. New alphabets have sometimes been introduced — the Initial Teaching Alphabet, for example, which is a phonetic alphabet designed to help English-speaking children to read, was in vogue in the nineteen sixties and seventies.

The pronunciation of most languages is to varying degrees imperfectly reflected in their alphabets. It is estimated, for example, that there are forty-two sounds in English; but the English alphabet has only twenty-six letters to represent them. This is in contrast to the classical language of India which is written in an alphabet which has characters for fourteen vowels and thirty-three simple consonants, plus two further symbols. This *Sanskrit,* or *Devanagari alphabet,* is a well-constructed one in which every letter has one invariable sound.

Although the advantages of an alphabetic system of writing may seem obvious to us, it should be remembered that this has not always been, and in some countries is still not, obvious to everyone. The more bureaucratic a government system, the less obvious the advantages are. Bureaucrats have a vested interest in a cumbersome, impenetrable system of writing, for if the population at large is able to read and write, their power is lessened. Such a system in any case took many centuries to evolve.

European languages use an alphabet which is descended from the Greek either directly or via the Roman alphabet, which itself was derived from the Greek. The Greeks, however, did not invent the alphabet. At the beginning of the ninth century BC they took it over ready-made from the Phoenicians. The Phoenicians themselves were merely using a variation of the writing used at that time by the Semites of Syria-Palestine — Canaanite writing. The names of the Canaanite letters, *'alef* (which means ox), *beth* (house), *gimel* (camel), *daleth* (door) etc. were adapted by the Greeks into *alpha, beta, gamma, delta* etc. The Canaanite letters were originally pictographs, with, for example, *'alef* being represented by the picture of an ox's head, *beth* by a simplified drawing of the ground plan of a house. From Canaanite the Semitic alphabets such as Hebrew and Arabic are descended; and we can see the progression to our own Roman letters in the table below:

| Egyptian | Proto-Semitic | Phoenician | Early Greek | Greek | Latin |
|---|---|---|---|---|---|
| | | | | | |
| 'alef | to | | alpha | to | A |
| | | | | | |
| beth | to | | beta | to | B |

The earliest-known version of the Canaanite alphabet is thought to have been developed about 1800 BC. In AD 1917, Alan Gardiner (1879-1963), a prominent English Egyptologist and philologist, was working on material from the site of an ancient Egyptian temple, dedicated to the goddess Hathor, at Serabit el-Khadim in the Sinai peninsula. Eleven of the inscriptions on which he was working resembled Egyptian hieroglyphs but were not Egyptian. Gardiner came to the conclusion that in these inscriptions lay the nucleus of an alphabetic writing-system, which he called "proto-Semitic". He put forward the theory that the inventor of this rudimentary alphabet must have been a Semite rather than an Egyptian. This theory he based on two facts. First, the goddess Hathor is called, in the Sinai inscriptions, *Ba'lat,* which is a Semitic term. Second, according to inscriptions at the site, when the turquoise mines at Serabit el-Khadim were exploited in Dynasty XII, Semites were employed there, mostly as miners. Hence Gardiner came to the conclusion that his "proto-Semitic" alphabet, from which all other alphabets are descended, was invented by a Semite, probably in the reign of the Twelfth-dynasty King of Egypt, Amenemhat III (*c.* 1842-1797 BC).

Although the "proto-Semitic" alphabet was developed under the aegis of the Egyptians, as it were, they themselves did not adopt the new invention. They continued as they had begun, with the much more cumbersome non-alphabetic system of writing which they had received from the Mesopotamians nearly fifteen hundred years before.

## How writing began: Mesopotamia

Mesopotamia lay in the plain between the two rivers, Tigris and Euphrates, roughly within the borders of modern Iraq. By 4000 BC southern Mesopotamia was inhabited by a race of farmers who had migrated from the north. These farmers, who were to be an important civilizing force in the Near East, are known as Ubaidians, a term derived from an archaeological excavation carried out some fifty years ago at one of their settlements near the ancient city of Ur, Tell el-Ubaid. Around the end of the fifth millennium BC hordes of Semitic nomads from the Syrian desert and the Arabian peninsula began to infiltrate the settlements of the non-Semitic Ubaidians. The subsequent cross-fertilisation of the two cultures laid the foundations of a new era in Mesopotamia.

About 3500 BC a third group of people arrived in Mesopotamia, possibly from Central Asia via Iran — the Sumerians. They were the builders of the world's first civilization. In the next thousand years or so the Sumerians reached unprecedented heights of achievement in art and architecture, social and political organisation, and religion, in creating an urban, literate society in southern Mesopotamia — Sumer. In 2300 BC, the Sumerian civilization came under the dominance of Sargon the Great, a Semite. He was the first ruler to unite Sumer with the northern half of Mesopotamia. This unified nation he ruled from a new city, Agade, which he built in a part of south-central Mesopotamia called Akkad. The Semitic language that was spoken in Mesopotamia from Sargon's time onwards is called Akkadian. It became the *lingua franca* of the ancient world.

The greatest achievement of the Sumerian civilization was the development of writing. Economic necessity seems to have been the mother of the invention of writing, for as the various cultures of the Near East became more prosperous and ever more complicated, the ruling classes found it essential that some record be kept of temple and palace property. It was until quite recently the accepted theory that writing had been invented in southern Mesopotamia; but evidence of the very earliest stages of writing has been found at several sites, notably at Susa in western Iran, Nineveh in Iraq and, in 1984, at Tell Brak in northern Syria. It seems likely, therefore, that writing was invented in several places at once, a not unreasonable proposition since the same impetus for the invention must have been present in more than one place.

The form and method of writing in Mesopotamia arose out of conditions in the country. The purpose of the writing was to record items of official property such as cattle, jars of wine, sacks of grain. Hence the writing took the form of simplified pictures of such items — pictographs. The method of writing was influenced by the materials available. Stone was scarce, papyrus and paper unknown: but clay was plentiful between the Tigris and the Euphrates. And so the first writing was done on wet clay moulded into small slabs known today as tablets, with a "pen" or stylus made from a reed whittled to a sharp point. When the writing was completed, the clay tablet was left to dry and harden in the sun. The pointed stylus was soon discarded in favour of a stylus with a triangular tip, which was pressed down into the clay, leaving wedge-shaped impressions in it. The Latin word for wedge — *cuneus* — has given this form of writing its name, *cuneiform writing*.

The earliest-known examples of Mesopotamian writing were found at Uruk, a site in southern Mesopotamia near the city of el-Ubaid. Uruk has eighteen stratigraphical levels: at Level IV, which can be dated to about 3500 BC, were found small tablets inscribed with pictographs of objects such as cows, sheep and cereals, scratched on the surface of the tablet with a pointed reed. Each object is accompanied by a series of signs shaped like strokes, circles and semicircles, presumably numerals. The purpose of the "writing" on the Uruk IV tablets is uncertain, but probably it was of an economic nature.

Gradually, the style and method of writing underwent changes. On the earliest tablets, the pictographs were scratched haphazardly onto the surface; no attempt seems to have been made to put the signs in straight lines or columns, either vertically or horizontally. Later, the pictographs were set down in vertical columns, usually beginning at the top right-hand corner of the tablet. By about 3250 BC the scribes had discovered that there was a tendency to smudge the text with their hands if they wrote in vertical columns; and so writing in vertical columns gave way to texts written horizontally, from left to right, top to bottom of the tablet. The pictographs themselves underwent a ninety degree turn. For instance, the sign for "ox", consisting of a simplified drawing of an ox's head which had been written , was now written .

In about 3000 BC, Sumerian writing underwent a change in content. For about five hundred years or so, it seems that writing had been confined to the use to which it had been put during the Uruk IV period. At two sites, Jemdat Nasr and Uruk III, dated *c.* 3000 BC, clay and stone tablets have been discovered which record lists of personal names (probably wage-lists), lists of objects or inventories, plus an assortment of economic texts such as receipts and memoranda. On these tablets, the objects depicted are no longer scratched with a pointed reed. Instead, an obliquely-cut reed-stem has been used and pressed down in the wet clay, resulting in the characteristic "wedges" of cuneiform writing. The pictograph becomes stylised; a scratched picture of an ox's head which was once written is now written .

**Development of Mesopotamian writing**

| Original pictograph | Later pictograph | Early cuneiform | Original or derived meaning |
|---|---|---|---|
| | | | bird |
| | | | fish |
| | | | ox |
| | | | sun, day |
| | | | grain |
| | | | to stand, to go |

The Sumerians went on to develop their writing until they achieved a system of such flexibility that people who spoke quite different languages such as Akkadian, Babylonian and Assyrian were able to adapt cuneifom to their own uses.

With the passage of time, cuneiform died out and was replaced by an alphabetic system which was derived from the "proto-Semitic" alphabet. The meaning of cuneiform script was lost for centuries. However, just as the mystery of Egyptian hieroglyphs was solved in the nineteenth century thanks to the Rosetta Stone, so the mystery of cuneiform writing was unravelled thanks to its own version of the Rosetta Stone.

Hewn into the face of a mountain in Behistun in Iran is an inscription of 1,306 lines which was carved on the instructions of Darius the Great, King of Persia, some 2,500 years ago. The inscription is in three languages — Old Persian, Elamite and Akkadian. In the nineteenth century, scholars were able to translate parts of the Old Persian inscription, and then, by comparing it with the other two, they were able to decipher the Elamite and the Akkadian, and thus "crack" the cuneiform writing.

# Chapter IV

## WRITING IN EGYPT

The pre-dynastic Egyptians lived in agricultural communities of an African rather than a western Asiatic character. It seems probable that the late pre-dynastic Egyptians were feeling their way towards an organised society that was largely agricultural but able to support several urban areas. They were forced to do so by an increase in population, by their growing prosperity and by the necessity to cooperate to take full advantage of the annual flooding of the Nile which brought life-giving water and fertile alluvium to an otherwise arid country.

A discernable and important stimulus to the development of Egyptian civilization occurred shortly before 3100 BC. Archaeological evidence points towards Mesopotamia as the source of that stimulus: Mesopotamian motifs are found in Egyptian art — composite animals, especially winged griffins and serpent-necked felines, pairs of entwined animals. A knife discovered at Gebel el-Arak in Upper Egypt (and now in the Louvre Museum) has a handle depicting, on one side, Mesopotamian-style ships, and on the other, a hero dominating two lions, the hero being dressed in Mesopotamian costume. In the architecture of their more important buildings — royal tombs, for example — the late-predynastic Egyptians began to use mud-brick arranged in recessed and panelled façades in the style that was used in Mesopotamia — the so-called "palace façade". Cylindrically-shaped seals were used by the Mesopotamians to impress their "signatures" on the wet clay tablets on which they wrote. Cylinder-seals have been discovered in Egypt, three of them apparently dating to the Mesopotamian Uruk IV period (*c.* 3500 BC). The Egyptians never used clay tablets: they simply used the seals as amulets.

The most important contribution made by Mesopotamia to early Egyptian civilization was *writing*. It seems probable that the idea of writing was introduced into Egypt by the

Sumerians shortly before 3100 BC. The Egyptians immediately adapted Mesopotamian pictographs into new forms which depicted objects that were of an Egyptian rather than Mesopotamian nature; and the earliest Egyptian hieroglyphic writing, found on slate cosmetic palettes of late pre-dynastic times, employs pictographs showing distinctively Egyptian objects. It gives the impression of being fully developed even at this early stage.

The Mesopotamians changed from picture writing to cuneiform script at an early date. They had had a tendency toward using abstract symbols from the outset; and cuneiform writing bears little resemblance to the original pictographs. The Egyptians, on the other hand, preferred the concrete to the abstract, and this is reflected in most of their hieroglyphic signs, which are exact illustrations of the objects they depict. As we shall see, hieroglyphic writing was later supplemented by hieratic and demotic scripts: but, in typical conservative Egyptian fashion, no script was abandoned in favour of another, and hieroglyphic writing was used from the outset until AD 394, when the last-known hieroglyphic inscription in Egypt was carved.

The purposes for which writing was used differed in Mesopotamia and Egypt. The Mesopotamians first used writing in a practical way, for administrative purposes. The Egyptians initially used writing as an adjunct to monumental art, one of the earliest examples being the Narmer palette. This commemorative slate palette is carved with reliefs showing the unification of Egypt under King Narmer, the founder of Dynasty I (*c.* 3100 BC). The top of one side of the palette is decorated with two faces of the cow-headed goddess, Hathor. Between the Hathor heads is written the name of Narmer, using two pictographs: one showing a cat-fish, the other a chisel. The ancient Egyptian word for cat-fish was *n'r* and the word for chisel was *mr.* Thus *n'r* and *mr* are two phonograms and are read *n'r-mr* (Narmer). The objects depicted in the pictographs are typically Egyptian rather than Mesopotamian.

From its inception in Egypt hieroglyphic writing seems to have consisted of a combination of ideograms (signs representing ideas) and phonograms (signs representing sounds) put together in a fairly complex way. Because phonograms had been introduced into the written language of ancient Egypt at an early stage, Egyptian hieroglyphic writing from the beginning was more than just simple picture writing.

The phonograms were identical in appearance to ideograms, but their meaning was extended. For instance, the sign ⬭ is the ideogram for r (mouth); however, ⬭ (r) can also be used as a phonogram. In the Egyptian language, the preposition "towards" has the same sound as the noun "mouth" (r, pronounced "ro" in each case): thus both words were represented by the same hieroglyph ⬭．The word for face was *hr* (pronounced "her") and was written with the sign 👁. The word for "on" was pronounced "her", and so it, too, was written with the sign 👁. In the same way, the word for "eye" was written ◉ and pronounced "an"; by the principle of rebus, the eye ◉ came to mean "beautiful" because the word for beautiful was *an*, and thus had the same sound as *an*, eye. Similarly, the hoe ⎺ (mer) was used for the verb mer, to love; the goose 🦆 (sa) was used to write sa, son; the beetle 🪲 (heper) was used to write heper, become; the lotus 🪷 (ha) was used to write ha, thousand.

In the examples given above, the words for face, eye, hoe, goose, beetle and lotus have been transliterated, that is, written in the Roman alphabet as her, an, mer, sa, heper and ha. From these transliterations it may be supposed that the Egyptians had at least two vowels (a and e). This is not the case: the transliterations above have been rendered with vowels in order to indicate pronunciation to the reader.

In common with other Semitic scripts, both ancient and modern, such as Phoenician, Hebrew and Arabic, the ancient Egyptians did *not* indicate vowel-sounds in their written script. The explanation for this phenomenon lies in the nature of Semitic languages where vowels are used in the *spoken* language simply to indicate modifications in the way groups of consonants, put together to make up words, are pronounced, since the pronunciation of the consonants determines the meaning of the word. The roots of the words, made up of consonants, do not change. It is easy, in these circumstances, to reach the conclusion that consonants are all that matters, that vowels are not important, and thus omit vowels in the*written* language. This can sometimes lead to serious misunderstandings; for example, the Arabic word قتل ˮ qtl, which can be read "qatal(a)" — "he killed" or "qutil(a)" — "he was killed" according to context. The ancient Egyptians must also have experienced such confusions.

In Indo-European languages, vowel sounds are as important as consonantal sounds. Thus when the Greeks adopted the Phoenician alphabet, they were forced to modify it by adding seven signs which represented vowels. The Phoenician alphabet was able to convey some vowel-sounds, but only if they were attached to consonants — *ba* or *be*, for example; and although the Phoenician *'aleph* became the vowel alpha in Greek, in Phoenician *'aleph* was a consonant. It is no exaggeration to claim that the seven Greek vowels have played a vitally important part in the history of literacy, for it is generally accepted today that vowels play a crucial part in the ease with which people learn to read.

Most words in the ancient Egyptian language were made up of groups of signs representing consonants which were written in hieroglyphs in a variety of *uniliteral*, *biliteral* or *triliteral* signs. The written language had twenty-four uniliteral signs each representing one consonant, a kind of "alphabet" which enabled the Egyptians to avoid using hundreds of other signs. The biliteral signs, by means of which the Egyptians could express two consonants in a single sign, and the triliteral signs, in which one hieroglyph stood for three consonants, also helped to avoid the necessity of using a vast number of signs. The written language had many ideograms and more than 150 phonograms.

Thus Egyptian hieroglyphs were an elaborate script which was capable of indicating phonetically all possible combinations of sounds in the Egyptian language. The Egyptians never developed the use of their "alphabetic" signs to the exclusion of all others. Only late on in their history did they display a preference for the use of alphabetic signs when writing royal names (e.g. Ptolemy, Kleopatra), or deliberately archaising inscriptions on public monuments.

The Egyptians used three *forms* of writing in the course of their history. They began with hieroglyphs; out of hieroglyphic writing there developed a more cursive script known as hieratic; and eventually, out of hieratic, a rapidly-written script known as demotic.

**Hieroglyphs or hieroglyphic writing.** The words "hieroglyph" and "hieroglyphic" are often used interchangeably, and are sometimes used incorrectly to describe the language of ancient Egypt. Strictly speaking, the word "hieroglyph" is a noun which should be used with reference to the *pictographic writing* of the ancient Egyptians, or indeed to the writing of any other people who employ pictographs. The term "hieroglyphic" is an adjective and should be used to describe the *mode* of writing. Thus it is correct to say "I can read hieroglyphs" or "I can read hieroglyphic writing"; but it is incorrect to say "I can read hieroglyphics". Neither is it correct to refer to the "hieroglyphic language". There is no such thing as a hieroglyphic language, only hieroglyphic writing. As far as ancient Egypt is concerned, the language is simply called "the ancient Egyptian language" or "ancient Egyptian". The language of modern Egypt is Arabic and is written in a non-pictographic script.

The term "hieroglyph" is derived from the Greek words *hieros* (sacred) *glupho* (sculptures), and was so called because by the time the Greeks first saw this oldest form of the writing of ancient Egypt it was being used almost exclusively for inscriptions on the walls of public monuments, especially temples. The ancient Egyptians themselves called their writing ⌐⎜ 𓄿 𓏏𓊹 *mdw ntr* ("medoo neter") "the god's words", the god referred to being Thoth, god of wisdom and inventor of writing.

In the beginning, hieroglyphic writing in Egypt was multi-purpose and used for literary, religious and monumental inscriptions on both hard and soft surfaces. Hieroglyphs were carved or painted on the walls of temples and tombs, on stone stelae, on wooden coffins and stone sarcophagi. They were written or painted on papyrus documents of a literary, religious, business or administrative nature. On the walls of temples, tombs and public monuments, the decorative effect of the hieroglyphs played an important part and they were often carved in elaborate detail and exquisitely coloured. When hieroglyphs were used on papyrus, however, they were from the outset drawn in a much abbreviated and utilitarian form. The use of hieroglyphs carved in stone persisted throughout Egyptian history until the last-known examples were carved in the Temple of Isis at Philae in AD 394.

Hieroglyphic writing was perfectly satisfactory for use on stone, where it was shaped with precision by a chisel. On papyrus, the use of a reed pen led to hieroglyphs being written rapidly in abbreviated and more rounded forms. Gradually, the use of hiero-glyphic writing became more and more confined to stone inscriptions, and was seldom used on papyrus for anything other than religious texts. A more cursive script was developed for use on materials other than stone. This script is called *hieratic.*

The word hieratic comes from the Greek *hieratikos,* meaning "priestly", so-called because by the Graeco-Roman period it was the script used almost exclusively by priests. When first introduced, hieratic was very like hieroglyphic writing in appearance: but from about 2000 BC it had a distinctive style of its own, and was used for any non-religious material written on papyrus. Hieroglyphs continued to be used for inscriptions on stone, and, until about 1000 BC, for religious texts written on papyrus. After that date, even religious texts on papyrus were written in hieratic.

The third type of script used by the ancient Egyptians was *demotic,* a term taken from the Greek *demotikos,* meaning popular. Demotic is a very abbreviated form of hieratic, almost on a par with shorthand. Its appearance has been likened to "a series of agitated commas"! It first came into use about 700 BC; and by the Graeco-Roman period it was the ordinary writing of everyday life for those people who knew how to write. The majority of the Egyptian populace was illiterate, relying on the services of professional scribes when it came to the reading and writing of letters, business documents or wills.

## The scribes

In ancient Egypt, the task of learning to read and write was not undertaken lightly. The Egyptians did not have the advantage of a wholly alphabetic system of writing, and in order to write fluently an Egyptian needed to learn hundreds of picture signs representing sounds, combinations of sounds and ideas. The minimum number of hieroglyphic signs required to write simple sentences is about 200. A list of signs used by a young Egyptian schoolboy has been found: it contains more than 450 characters. At a more advanced stage he would have needed about 750 signs; and a competent scribe would have known several hundred more.

It is not surprising, therefore, that few Egyptians could read or write. The average Egyptian was a peasant farmer, or his wife, with little or no interest beyond the confines of their own village, his energies being expended on growing his crops and tending his animals, hers on household duties. They had neither the inclination nor the opportunity, nor, since professional scribes were plentiful, the need, to learn to write.

In an illiterate country such as Egypt, the man who could read and write was considered greatly superior to his fellow men. In a bureaucratic country such as Egypt, the scribe was master. He was a member of a profession which was "the foremost of all professions". The office of scribe was the opening to bigger and better things. The great Amenhotep, son of Hapu, was scribe to his king, Amenhotep III (called Amenophis by the Greeks): he had reached one of the highest offices to which a noble could aspire, that of Scribe to the King.

The profession of scribe was not the exclusive preserve of the nobility. Even a boy of lowly origin could become a scribe, provided his family could afford to send him to school, or find him a rich sponsor. The difficulty lay not in the cost of school fees, but rather to the fact that a peasant family could not afford the loss of a child's labour. Schools were usually attached to temples. Boys (very seldom girls) were sent there from the age of four or five. They were often boarders, although the school did not provide food. Instead, servants or mothers would have to visit the school daily bringing supplies of the bread and beer which formed the staple diet of the ancient Egyptians. The main subjects taught were reading, writing, arithmetic, geography and history; and the object of education was to train boys to be clerks in local and government offices, to give them sufficient basic knowledge for entry into the priesthood, and to train them to be artists and draughtsmen.

Writing exercises were done on small pieces of stone or broken pottery (sherds) which were thrown away after use. This habit has proved invaluable to Egyptology. On occasion sherds are found on which schoolboys have practised writing by copying out a well-known story which has otherwise survived only in a version on a damaged or incomplete papyrus. Thanks to these schoolboy exercises Egyptologists are sometimes able to fill in gaps in the narrative.

One of the most common exercises a schoolboy had to copy out was an exhortation to him to work hard. This served the dual purpose of improving his writing and subtly working on his mind:

Work hard every day. Thus shall you obtain mastery over

writing. Spend not a day in idleness or you will be beaten.

The ear of a boy is on his back — he listens when he is

beaten!

It can be seen from this exercise that the Egyptians subscribed to the Wackford Squeers school of educational theory!

Should boys be tempted by another way of life, model "letters" from fathers might be given to them to copy out; for example:

I am told ... that your thoughts stray to work on the farm, and that you turn your back on writing. Do you not realise how the husbandman fares when the harvest is registered (for taxation purposes)? The worm has taken half the corn, the hippopotamus has devoured the rest. The mice abound in the field and the locust has descended. The cattle eat constantly, and the sparrows steal. Woe betide the husbandman! But the scribe! He is the one who directs the work of everybody. For him there are no taxes, for he pays tribute by writing, and there are no dues for him.

What do you mean by saying, "The soldier is considered to be better off than the scribe"? Let me tell you how woefully the soldier fares. His superiors are many ... He is woken up after only an hour's sleep. He is driven like an ass. He works until the sun goes down. He is dead while yet alive ... If he returns home (after a campaign) he is like worm-eaten wood. He is sick and becomes bedridden ... Forget the idea that the soldier is better off than the scribe!

The picture these "letters" give of the misery endured by men who take up professions other than that of scribe is, of course, biased and exaggerated. Nevertheless, the profession of scribe was the most important one in Egypt. It was the influential scribes who moulded Egyptian thought and maintained standards throughout Egyptian history.

Their names abide forever ... their names are pronounced because of the books they have made. Be a scribe, put it in your heart, that your name might fare likewise. More profitable than a graven tombstone is a book.

## The scribe's materials and tools

The Egyptians used many kinds of material on which to write: stone, wood, metal, parchment, vellum, leather. But the writing material which set them apart from other ancient peoples, and gave them such an advantage, was *papyrus*. Whereas, for instance, the Mesopotamians were forced to use baked clay, which could be cumbersome and heavy, on which to write because they had no other material readily available to them, the Egyptians had the enormous advantage of a light, smooth material, papyrus. Papyrus was made from narrow strips of the pith of fresh green papyrus-plant (*Cyperus papyrus*) stems. Two layers of strips were placed together at right angles, pressed and pounded into a flat sheet. Several sheets of papyrus could be joined together to make a roll of papyrus: the sheets were never more than about 43 cms wide and about 48 cms high; the longest roll so far known is the Great Harris Papyrus (now in the British Museum) which is 41 m long.

The word papyrus has given us our word paper; paper, however, is made of wood, cotton or linen fibres, and was invented in China. Papyrus plants once grew in profusion in the Nile valley and were used for many purposes other than "paper" making — for boats, skiffs, ropes, baskets, sandals, fences, mats. A sad fact is that, today, papyrus no longer grows in the wild in Egypt but only in plant nurseries; and in a pool in the courtyard of the Egyptian Museum in Cairo.

The Egyptian word for scribe is *šs* ("sesh-es") and means "he who writes"; it is written [hieroglyphic sign]. The hieroglyphic sign illustrates the three tools of the scribal trade. First, the rectangular palette, usually made of wood or alabaster, with two bowls containing cakes of "ink". A scribe's "ink" took the form of round, dry cakes of colour, usually black (carbon) or red (ochre). On papyrus, the red "ink" served to highlight rubrics in a sentence; on stone, it was used to correct mistakes in hieroglyphs which had been sketched out in black ready for carving. Second, the pot, containing a light gum which was used to help the "ink" adhere to the writing surface. Third, the holder for "pens". The "pens" were actually brushes made from reeds. The most popular reed for use as a brush was a *Phragmites communis.* Its stem was trimmed to between 15 and 25 cms in length, and one end was cut on a slant and then chewed by the scribe to fray it so that it would take up the "ink" more readily. A scribe would moisten his "pen" every so often with the gum, brush it across the cake of "ink" and apply it to the writing material. A string connected the three tools so that they could be carried in the scribe's hand or slung over his shoulder.

The status in society enjoyed by scribes is reflected in the fact that many of them could afford to have statues made of themselves; and in the fact that they are proud to have these statues depict them in the characteristic pose of the scribe — seated cross-legged upon the ground, wearing a kilt. The kilt is stretched taut across the knees thus providing a "desk" on which to rest a papyrus-roll. The face of the scribe in such statues, especially the eyes, has an alert and eager expression as the scribe prepares to "direct the affairs of everyone".

**Chapter V**

## THE LANGUAGE OF THE ANCIENT EGYPTIANS

A language normally has affinities with several other tongues which, grouped together, form a family. English, for instance, belongs to the Indo-European family which also includes the languages of modern Russia, ancient Turkey (Hittite) and ancient India (Sanskrit). The language of ancient Egypt belongs to the so-called Hamito-Semitic family. The term "Hamitic" refers to the African group of languages. According to Genesis X one of Noah's sons went forth after the Flood and became the ancestor of the African tribes. From the name of this son, Ham, is the word Hamitic derived. The word Semitic comes from the name of another of Noah's sons, Shem, who was traditionally the ancestor of the Aramean, Phoenician and Assyrian races; and, ironically, of both the Hebrews and the Arabs.

The origin of the ancient Egyptian language is not precisely known. It is thought to have elements of the Hamitic group of languages spoken in north-east Africa, such as Berber, Galla and Somali: over a hundred Egyptian words have roots in common with words in these Hamitic tongues. Ancient Egyptian was also influenced by the Semitic languages: over three hundred words have been traced in which the Egyptian word has roots in common with the Semitic. Thus the linguistic background of the language of the ancient Egyptians is, as far as can be deduced, much the same as their supposed racial origins — a mixture of African and Semitic.

The language of ancient Egypt should not be confused with that spoken in Egypt today, which is Arabic. Arabic was introduced into Egypt after the country was conquered by invaders from the Arabian Peninsula, the Muslim Arabs. Within a year of the Prophet Mohammad's death in AD 632, the religious zeal of his followers led to the expansion of Islam through conquest of new territories; and by 681 the Arab empire stretched from northern Africa and the Near East almost to the borders of India. The conquest of Egypt began in 639 and was completed in 642.

The ancient Egyptians began their written records shortly before 3100 BC and continued with the use of hieroglyphs, later supplemented by hieratic and demotic, until the Christian era. Unfortunately, it is only from these written records that we know ancient Egyptian, and so we cannot be sure how the language was spoken. Attempts to reconstruct the sound of ancient Egyptian are greatly handicapped by the fact that vowel sounds were not written down. Any written group of consonants could have been pronounced using one or more vowel sounds before, between or after, the letters forming the group. For instance, the word for "sky" is written in Egyptian using the hieroglyphs for the consonants *p* and *t*. Is *pt* to be pronounced "epet", "opet", "pot", "pat", "peet", "puat", "peti", "pata", etc. etc.? In other words, where do the vowels go! We shall see later how this problem can partially be solved.

The civilization of ancient Egypt lasted for over three thousand years. It is to be expected that over such a period of time many changes in the grammar, vocabulary and pronunciation of the language would occur. The Egyptians were an intensely conservative people; hence their language and customs changed very slowly. But change they did. On several occasions, the changes were given impetus by outside influences: in the fifteenth century BC, for instance, Egypt established an empire in the Near East. One of the results of this was an influx of Near Eastern customs and ideas into Egypt; and a variety of non-Egyptian words were introduced into the Egyptian language.

Any language is bound to change as the centuries go by. It is not necessary to go back as far as the Old English that displaced the Celtic language in England in the fifth century AD; or to the Norman English that was spoken for several centuries after the Conquest of 1066, to realise that profound changes have occurred in the English language in the last six hundred years alone. Modern English, for example, is different from the Victorian English spoken in the time of Charles Dickens, a fact that was made amply clear in 1961 when volcanic eruptions forced the inhabitants of a group of remote islands in the South Atlantic, Tristan da Cunha, to seek refuge in Britain for a time. The islanders of Tristan da Cunha had been largely out of contact with the outside world since the nineteenth century; and on arrival in Britain the descendants of the original Victorian settlers were heard to speak in the Cockney used by Sam Weller in *The Pickwick Papers*. Their vocabulary included many Victorian words and usages which have disappeared from modern English.

Victorian English was, in turn, different from that of Elizabethan times, exemplified by Shakespeare. And the fourteenth-century English of Chaucer, spoken less than six hundred years ago, is almost like a foreign language to us today. Take, for example, the first lines of the Prologue to his *Canterbury Tales:*

> When that Aprille with his shoures sote
> The Droghte of Marche hath perced to the rote,
> And bathed every veyne in swich licour
> Of which vertu engendered is the flour ...
> Than longen folk to goon on pilgrimages ...

Since Chaucer's time, the words used by him have changed their meaning, fallen out of use, changed their spelling, as spoken English has evolved to what it is today. So, too, did ancient Egyptian evolve.

The spoken language of Egypt changed more rapidly than the written, a common phenomenon. At times, spoken Egyptian was in step with the written language; at other times, the written language lagged behind the spoken until an attempt was made to bridge the gap. At all times, monumental records on stone were more conservative than business documents or letters written on papyrus. The same sort of difference can be noted in English, where a letter written to a friend tends to be couched in very different language from that used in, for instance, the law courts, which have a tendency to employ an English that uses archaic, legalistic terms.

There is a Hindu proverb which states that "language changes every eighteen or twenty miles". Whilst this is very much an exaggeration as far as ancient Egypt was concerned, spoken Egyptian did have regional dialects, although very little written Egyptian reflects them, at least until the Christian era. It is possible that there was a distinctive pronunciation of the language spoken at Court, on a par with the standardised and preferred pronunciation of the English language which was developed in Victorian England so that a speaker might be identified as someone who belonged to the professional middle class. R.P. or Received Pronunciation was also an indication that a speaker was fit to be received at Court — a stricture which would have disqualified Samuel Johnson, perhaps the most eminent literary figure of the eighteenth century — Dr Johnson spoke with a Staffordshire accent! In a hierarchical country such as ancient Egypt, it is tempting to think that a paraphrase of George Bernard Shaw's dictum would be apt: "it is impossible for an [Egyptian] to open his mouth without making some other [Egyptian] despise him." [*Pygmalion,* Preface].

Egyptologists have been able to discern four main stages in the development of the Egyptian language:

1. *Old Egyptian:* the language used from Dynasty I to Dynasty VI (*c.* 3100-2180 BC). Known mainly from religious texts inscribed in the pyramids of five kings of Dynasties V and VI (the Pyramid Texts) and from captions to the reliefs painted or sculpted on the walls inside the tombs of nobles, or from the biographies of the owners of these tombs engraved at the entrance to, or inside, the tomb.

2. *Middle Egyptian:* the language which came into use between Dynasty XI and Dynasty XII (2134-1786 BC). Regarded by Egyptian scribes as the classic stage of their language, it remained their ideal model until Roman times. Middle Egyptian is a grammatically strict and balanced language in which, for a time, the written word was similar to the spoken. Written Middle Egyptian was used for religious texts, narratives, poetry, business and administrative documents. Eventually, however, its use was reserved for historical and religious inscriptions on stone or papyrus. It was revived in the Graeco-Roman period and employed for temple inscriptions, where it was written in a cryptic and decorative script known as Ptolemaic.

3. *Late Egyptian*: the vernacular used from the end of Dynasty XVIII until Dynasty XXIV (1300-715 BC). Late Egyptian differs in syntax, grammar and vocabulary

from Middle Egyptian, and the spoken language seems to have differed a great deal from the written. Evidence of this is found in letters, maxims and stories where colloquialisms, which were avoided in official documents, have crept in.

4. *Coptic:* the Egyptian language in its latest form, much changed from Old Egyptian. Used from third to seventh century AD when it was superceded by Arabic as the official language of the country. It is invaluable in the study of the language of ancient Egypt because, unlike ancient Egyptian, its vowel-sounds are written down, thus giving a clearer indication of how words were pronounced.

## The Copts and Coptic

In 332 BC Alexander the Great conquered Egypt. From then on, until the Roman conquest in 30 BC, Egypt was under the control of Hellenistic rulers. The Thirty-second and last dynasty of kings to rule Egypt before the coming of Christ was not Egyptian but Macedonian Greek. The official language of the country during this period, the language spoken by the ruling classes and by educated persons, was Greek. The peasants spoke in the same tongue as their ancestors, although in a form which differed even more from the original Egyptian than modern English differs from Chaucer's. These descendants of the ancient Egyptians are called "Copts"; the language they spoke is called "Coptic".

The term "Copt" comes from the Greek "Aiguptos" — Egypt. This became *qibt* in Arabic and Copt in English. Originally, the term Copt simply meant a native of Egypt; eventually, however, the term was reserved for reference to the Christian inhabitants of Egypt. This meaning of the word was first employed in Europe in the sixteenth century AD.

For a long time, the Copts kept their language, which was spoken in several dialects. By AD 290, when Egypt had become a Roman province and formed part of Rome's eastern empire, Christianity had spread throughout the Near East. The Christian Copts of Egypt wanted to write down the Bible, especially the Gospels, in their own language. However, their written language, consisting as it did of hieroglyphs, hieratic and demotic scripts, was not well suited to the task, the main disadvantage being the lack of written vowel sounds which would prevent an exact translation of Christian teachings being made.

The Copts solved the problem by adapting the Greek alphabet for their purposes by adding seven new signs to it to cover sounds not found in Greek. Thus Coptic is the latest form of the ancient Egyptian language written not in hieroglyphs, hieratic or demotic but in Greek letters. Problems such as the one outlined above where the correct pronunciation of the word for sky, *pt*, was discussed, can be solved with the aid of Coptic. In ancient Egyptian, "sky" is written ⌐□ △⌐ (the upper signs are uniliteral hieroglyphic signs, the lower sign is a determinative). In Coptic, the word is written πε. From this we can deduce that the ancient Egyptian consonants *p* and *t* should have the vowel "e" placed between them in pronunciation, giving "pet" as the spoken Egyptian for "sky".

The first truly Coptic writings appeared around the third century AD. Over the next two centuries, a greater use of Coptic writing coincided with the growth of the Egyptian Christian church, the development of monasteries, the disappearance of hieroglyphs, and the decline of Greek influence in Egypt combined with an upsurge of Egyptian, and therefore Coptic, nationalism. In art and architecture a distinctively Coptic style developed, different from the Pharaonic style and much influenced by Byzantine and Romanesque forms. The most original literary documents were the work of monks, men such as St Anthony and St Pachom. Anthony, who was born *c.* AD 251, and Pachom, who was born *c.* AD 292, were the founders of the monastic system as it is known in the West today. Their writings were mostly epistles, biographies of the Saints, and rules for their monasteries. The most nationalistic of the Coptic monks was Shenute, who was born in AD 334. He took over from his uncle, Bgoul, as Head of the White Monastery at Sohag in Upper Egypt when he was fifty-one years old; and by the time he died in 452, apparently at the age of 118 years, he had produced such a large amount of written work that he is considered to be the foremost Coptic literary figure.

The year before Shenute's death, in AD 451, the Council of Ephesus had been held. The result of the Council was the adoption by the Christian Church of the belief that Christ had two natures, one human and one divine. Thanks in part to nationalism, the Coptic Church clung to the Monophysite heresy — the belief that Christ had one, wholy divine, nature. The Coptic Church broke away from the rest of Christendom; and Egypt suffered years of religious conflict between orthodox and Coptic Christians. After the Arab Conquest in the seventh century Coptic Christians began to decline in number. Many converted to Islam; Coptic churches and monasteries were abandoned; in the tenth century, the last great Coptic scriptoria were closed. Eventually, most of Egypt was Arabic-speaking and Muslim. Enclaves of Christian Egyptians, Copts, remained. They also spoke Arabic in everyday life; but they continued to use Coptic in their Church liturgy, rather as Latin was used until recently in the Roman Catholic Church, although the use of Coptic generally had died out by the sixteenth century.

The Coptic language seems to have had five main dialects, each derived from the speech of a particular part of the country: (i) Fayumic, used in the district around the Fayum Depression in the Western Desert; (ii) Akhmimic, used in the region of the town of Akhmim in Upper Egypt; (iii) Sub-Akhmimic, possibly used in the locality of Assiut, Upper Egypt; (iv) Bohairic, possibly used in Memphis and the Delta; and (v) Sahidic, used in the district of Thebes (modern-day Luxor) in Upper Egypt. Sahidic is the classical literary form of the language, made so largely thanks to the literary output of Shenute (see above); Bohairic is the dialect used in present-day Church liturgy.

Today, about one-seventh of the population of Egypt is Coptic. Few Copts can actually speak, read, write or understand Coptic; and their numbers are perhaps insufficient to ensure the survival for much longer of this last, tenuous, link with the language of Pharaonic Egypt.

## The survival of ancient Egyptian words in modern languages

In spite of the persistence of the ancient Egyptian language through several millennia, and in spite of the influence Egypt exercised on neighbouring countries — Nubia and the Sudan to the south, Libya to the west, Syria and Palestine to the north-east (ruled by Egypt for centuries), and other countries adjacent to Syria-Palestine with whom Egypt maintained relations, warlike and otherwise — the language of ancient Egypt has left a surprisingly small mark on the languages of the world.

This might be expected in the cases of Nubia and the Sudan, and of Libya, because the ancient native languages of these countries have no written records and were superceded by the languages of invaders who came after the Egyptians. It is, however, more surprising in the countries to the north-east of Egypt. The Semites of these regions have left written records almost as old as those of ancient Egypt; in the case of Mesopotamia, even older. We know from the story of a famous Egyptian traveller, Wenamun, that around 1085 BC he met a man from as far away as Cyprus who could speak Egyptian. And yet, scarcely a hundred years later, when the oldest parts of the Bible were being written, very few Egyptian words were remembered.

Of the rich and varied Egyptian vocabulary of over 20,000 words, only five are found for certain in the Bible. Two of these words are measures of capacity: *ephah* from the Egyptian *ipt* (18 litres) and *hin* from the Egyptian *hnw* (a jar). The word *pharaoh* comes from the Greek pharao, which in turn comes from the Hebrew, par'o. In Egyptian, the term is *pr '3* (pronounced per aar) which means "the Great House", a way of referring to the king by identifying him with the Royal Palace. Although we now tend to call the kings of Egypt "Pharaohs", the Egyptians themselves did not always do so. Until Dynasty XVIII, the phrase *pr '3* simply referred to the royal palace; the earliest-known example of the term being employed to describe the king himself is found in a letter written to Akhenaten (Amenhotep IV), the husband of the famous Nefertiti, in about 1360 BC.

Two personal names found in the Bible are Egyptian in origin: *ššn* - lotus — became *shushan* (lily) in Hebrew, then the name Shushanna, which became Sousanna in Greek and Susanna(h) to us. *Petepre* (He-whom-(the god) Re-has-given) in Egyptian became Potiphar in the Bible. The most famous Biblical character to have connections with Egypt is Moses. Egyptian had a word *msw* , which means "born"; there is some doubt, however, as to whether this can be read "Moses" since in Hebrew Moses is written with a different s from that in *msw*.

Several Egyptian words have come down to us from the Greek. The Egyptian *hbny* was a tree which grew in Nubia and had hard, black wood: in Greek, *hbny* became *ebenos*, which in turn became ebony in English. In Egyptian, *ḳmyt* was the sap from the acacia tree: *ḳmyt* became *kommi* in Greek, *gummi* in Latin, *gum* in English. In Egyptian, the word *s3k* meant a receptacle or holder of some sort. In Greek, the word became *sakkos,* in Latin, *saccus,* in English, *sack.*

The worlds of geography, chemistry and geology owe some words to the Egyptians. The Greek word *oasis* is of Egyptian derivation: the original word was *wḥ3t* (pronounced "waa het"), the literal meaning of which is "cauldron". The gas *ammonia* and the fossil *ammonite* are both derived from the name of one of Egypt's most powerful gods, Amun. There was a temple and an oracle of Amun at the Siwa oasis in the Western Desert. The most famous person to consult the oracle of Amun at Siwa was Alexander the Great: and after Alexander, Greeks and Romans continued to honour Amun, whom they called Zeus Ammon and Jupiter Ammon respectively. *Sal ammoniacus* (ammoniac salt) was found near the temple at Siwa, hence the term "ammonia". The animal held sacred to Amun was a ram, hence Amun was often depicted wearing ram's horns; and it is its resemblance to these horns that has earned the fossil *ammonite* its name.

Our legacy of ancient Egyptian words is small. Even the Inuit (Eskimos), whose language was written down less than two hundred years ago, have given us words such as kayak, nunatak, igloo, anorak, parka, almost as many as the ancient Egyptians have given with their three thousand years of written history.

The final blow to ancient Egyptian linguistic pride comes when one realises that even things that are famously associated with Egypt are not now referred to by their Egyptian names. What could be more Egyptian than pyramids, obelisks and mummies; or the famous Sphinx at Giza? Yet the words we use for these things are not Egyptian; and in most cases demonstrate the truth of the saying "the Greeks have a word for it". In Egyptian, the word for pyramid was *mr*; our word "pyramid" comes from the name of the little Greek cakes made of wheat and honey and shaped like pyramids — *puramides.* The Egyptian word for obelisk was *thn;* the English word comes from the Greek *obeliskoi -*

the small spits on which meat etc. was cooked. The Greeks did not have a word for mummy. The Egyptian word was *s'ḥ*. The Persian word for the tarry substance, bitumen, with which mummified bodies of the Late Period were covered, is *mumiya*: hence the term "mummy".

As for the *Sphinx*. The ancient Egyptians had many sphinxes. They were normally represented as lions with the head of a king, although occasionally they were sphinxes of queens, with a queen's head upon the body of a lioness. Sometimes sphinxes took the form of a panther with a falcon's head which trampled upon the enemies of the King of Egypt; and sometimes sphinxes were surmounted by the head of an animal particularly associated with a certain god. This is the case at Karnak, Luxor, where there is a double row of sphinxes leading up to the Temple of Amun: each of these sphinxes has the head of the ram which was sacred to Amun. None of these Egyptian sphinxes was cruel. An Egyptian sphinx was a manifestation of divinity and royalty: its purpose was to protect tombs and temples, and to overcome enemies.

The most renowned, the largest and oldest of Egyptian sphinxes is at Giza, near Cairo. It is nearly 74 m long and up to 20 m high and was carved out of a limestone knoll in Dynasty IV, some 4,500 years ago, in front of the second-largest pyramid of the three which together formed one of the Seven Wonders of the Ancient World. Its face is the face of King Khafre (known to the Greeks as Chephren), before whose pyramid the Great Sphinx was built. In the New Kingdom, the Sphinx of Giza was identified with a form of the sun-god and called "Harmachis" (Horus-on-the-Horizon).

The Egyptian word for "sphinx" is *šspw;* but in spite of the fame of the great *šspw* at Giza it is, once again, a Greek word — sphinx — that is used to describe it. The story of Oedipus shows that the Greeks themselves had a sphinx which was in the shape of a winged lioness with a woman's head. Unlike the Egyptian sphinxes, this sphinx had a cruel nature and asked for answers to riddles on pain of death. The now-famous saying "the riddle of the sphinx" refers to the riddle asked by the Greek sphinx, which was:

What goes on four feet, on two feet, and three,

But the more feet it goes on the weaker it be?

To which Oedipus gave the answer that it was a man, who in infancy crawls upon all fours, in manhood goes upright on two feet, and in old age needs the support of a third "leg", a staff. Upon hearing this, the correct answer, the sphinx killed herself.

Even the words for the river Nile and for Egypt itself are not Egyptian. The Greeks called Egypt's great river by the general Semitic term for river, *nahal,* from which the English word, Nile, is derived. The ancient Egyptians themselves called it *ḥ'py.* The most popular name for Egypt as used by the ancient Egyptians was *kmt* or *keme* (the Black Land, a reference to the alluvial soil deposited by the annual Nile inundation). This became *al kimia* in Arabic, then alchemy and chemistry in English. The English words arose out of a confusion between the Arabic name for Egypt and the science which Europeans credited the Arabs with inventing — alchemy. The English word Egypt is derived from the Greek *Aiguptos.* This in turn came from the Egyptian *ḥwt-k3-Ptḥ* - Mansion of the Ka (or soul) of Ptah (the creator-god of Memphis). The *ḥwt-k3-Ptḥ* was the name of the great temple of Ptah in Memphis, the ancient capital city of Egypt; but the name of the temple was extended by the Greeks to encompass the whole of Egypt.

The debt that the modern world owes to ancient Egypt lies not in the legacy of words from the Egyptian language, which is a pitifully small number, but for the fact that it was an Egyptian invention, papyrus, which enabled the great works of Greek and Roman literature to be transmitted and preserved, eventually to be inherited by us.

# PART II

## Grammar, exercises and vocabularies

This section of 'Introducing Egyptian hieroglyphs' aims to supply the reader with enough basic grammar and vocabulary for him to be able to attempt translations of simple Middle Egyptian texts and inscriptions.

It is arranged in eleven Lessons, at the end of each of which is a Vocabulary and a set of Exercises for the student to practise what he has learned in the preceding Lesson.

A Key to the Exercises will be found at the back of the book; so, also, will a glossary of all the words used in the Exercises. This is arranged under two headings—an Egyptian-English Vocabulary and an English-Egyptian Vocabulary.

A sign-list of the hieroglyphic signs used in Part II appears on pages 125-136.

# PART II

## Grammar, exercises and vocabularies

## LESSON 1

### Direction of hieroglyphic writing

Hieroglyphic writing is a decorative script; scribes were at great pains to arrange the signs in an artistic way with no unsightly gaps or ugly groupings.

Inscriptions were written either in horizontal lines or in vertical columns (from top to bottom). In both cases the lines and the columns, and the individual signs within them, could be written either from right to left or from left to right. It has become the custom for modern printed books to adapt all hieroglyphic inscriptions so that when printed they are read from left to right, even though the original inscription may be read otherwise. This is done in order to simplify the reading of hieroglyphs when they accompany a western language.

The different directions in which hieroglyphs can be written are especially noticeable in inscriptions carved in stone where a decorative effect was being sought. For instance, inscriptions written around doorways can reflect the Egyptians' love of symmetry. Often, the same inscription is written on each side of an entrance. In order to keep a balance, the hieroglyphs on the left-hand side are written so that they face the doorway, and those on the right-hand side do likewise. The inscriptions above the doorway are divided into two halves, both equal in length and identical to look at, except that the signs on the right-hand side of the centre-point are read from left to right, and those on the left-hand side are read from right to left.

When reading a hieroglyphic inscription, the reader has first to decide the sequence in which the signs are to be read. There is an easy way to do this: observe the direction in which the signs depicting living things (human or animal) are facing. In nearly all cases, they will face the beginning of the inscription. The reader should therefore read *towards the faces* of living things. For example, the words  must be read from left to right because the snake, the bird and the man all face towards the left.

In lines of hieroglyphs, and in the signs within the lines, upper has precedence over lower. For example, in the word ⟨glyphs⟩ the order of signs is ⟨glyph⟩ + ⟨glyph⟩ + ⟨glyph⟩ + ⟨glyph⟩ + ⟨glyph⟩ + ⟨glyph⟩ , + ⟨glyph⟩

The following examples illustrate the four possible ways of reading hieroglyphs. In each case, the arrows show the direction in which the writing is to be read ; the letters give the order of the lines ; and the numbers indicate the sequence of the individual signs.

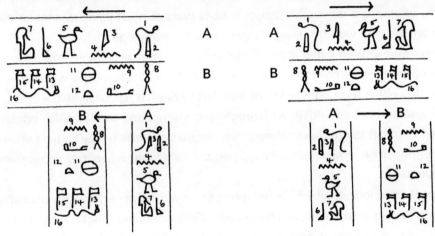

Note that the hieroglyphs are not divided into individual words ; and that no punctuation signs are used.

## Pronunciation

The Ancient Egyptian language, in common with Semitic languages such as Hebrew and Arabic, did not express its vowel sounds in written form. The reason for this is easy to find. It is a characteristic of the Semitic family of languages that words are pronounced differently according to grammatical use or context. For instance, the Egyptian word for house ⟨glyph⟩ may have been pronounced 'par' when used in isolation, 'per' when followed by a genitive, 'epraru' when used in the plural. In languages where vowels are changed to indicate the uses of words, it is easy to assume that consonants are all that matter; hence, in the written language, vowels are not indicated.

In Egyptian, the word for sky is written ⎯. We know that ⊓ is *p* and ⌒ is *t*. The ⎯ is a sign which indicates the meaning of the first two signs. It is called a determinative and is not pronounced. Egyptian has many of these signs (see page 66). *p* and *t* are two consonants. In general, consonants by themselves are not pronounceable. The problem of pronouncing several of them strung together to make a word has been solved by Egyptologists by the expedient of inserting an 'e' wherever there seems to be a need for a vowel. Hence, the *p* and *t* of the word 'sky' are usually pronounced 'pet'.

In this instance, the pronunciation is probably close to the way in which the Ancient Egyptians pronounced the word. We know that in Coptic, the word for sky is ⊓≺ , pronounced 'pay'. It can be deduced from this that the Middle Egyptian word *pt* was pronounced 'pet'. The final letter of the word, *t*, had fallen away by the time the word had reached the Coptic period. This is because, like the English letter g, the Egyptian letter *t* is weak. In both languages, weak letters placed at the ends of words tend to fall away. For example, in English, getting can become gettin'; going become goin'.

## Transliteration

When translating Egyptian texts, the beginner will find it useful to *transliterate* them before attempting a *translation*. Transliteration in this instance means turning the hieroglyphic signs into an approximation of English alphabetic signs. Thus, the sentence used above in our example of writing direction is *transliterated* and *translated* as follows:

| *Transliteration* | ḏd mdw in Gb ḥn' psḏt.f |
| --- | --- |
| *Translation* | For recitation by Geb and his Ennead |
|  | (see Vocabulary 1 below) |

## The alphabet

The Egyptians never adopted an entirely alphabetic system of writing. They did, however, have an alphabet, consisting of twenty-four letters, which they used with their many other signs, their phonograms and ideograms. The letters of the Egyptian alphabet are listed below. At first glance some of the letters in transliteration look similar to some of the vowels used in English. It should be remembered, however, that Ancient Egyptian had no written vowels.

## The alphabet

| Sign | Transliteration | Object depicted | Approximate pronunciation |
|------|-----------------|-----------------|---------------------------|
| 𓄿 | 3 | vulture | a as in father |
| 𓇋 | ỉ | flowering reed | i as in filled |
| 𓇌 (or \\) | y | two reeds | y as in discovery |
| 𓂝 | ˀ | arm & hand | a as in car |
| 𓅱 | w | quail chick | oo as in too<br>also w as in wet |
| 𓃀 | b | foot | b as in boot |

| Sign | Transliteration | Object depicted | Approximate pronunciation |
|------|-----------------|-----------------|---------------------------|
| ▱ | p | stool | p as in pedestal |
| ♒ | f | horned viper | f as in feel |
| 🦉 | m | owl | m as in moon |
| ∿∿∿ | n | water | n as in noon |
| ⬯ | r | mouth | r as in right |
| ⌐⌐ | h | reed shelter | h as in hat |
| § | ḥ | wick of twisted flax | h as in ha ! |
| ⊘ | ḫ | placenta (?) | ch as in loch |
| ☀⬯ | ẖ | animal's belly with teats | ch as in German ich |
| (i) ⌐  (ii) ―╫― | s | (i) folded cloth (ii) door bolt | s as in saw |
| ▭ | š | pool | sh as in show |

| Sign | Transliteration | Object depicted | Approximate pronunciation |
|------|-----------------|-----------------|---------------------------|
| ᕦ | ḳ | hill-slope | like q in queen |
| ᑌ | k | basket with handle | k as in basket |
| 𓎼 | g | jar stand | g as in go |
| ᑎ | t | loaf | t as in tap |
| ᖇ | ṯ | tethering rope | like ch in church |
| ᕥ | d | hand | d as in dog |
| ᒉ | ḏ | snake | dj as in adjust |

## Notes on the alphabet

Since we do not know how the Egyptians named the letters of their alphabet, the hieroglyps 𓄿 ꜣ, 𓇋 ỉ and 𓂝 ꜥ have been given Hebrew names. ꜣ is ʼaleph, ỉ is yodh and ꜥ is ʼayin.

The aleph, 𓄿, although pronounced like the a in father, is not a vowel but a weak consonant.

The yodh, 𓇋, should not be confused with the English i; although at first glance the yodh looks like a lower case English i, careful inspection of the transliteration of the sign will show that the dot on the i has been replaced by a ͻ.

The hieroglyphs ꜣ *i* and ꜣ *w* are consonants which bear a close resemblance to the English vowels i and u; hence they are known as semi-vowels.

## Vocabulary to Lesson 1

*ḏd mdw* (djed medoo) for recitation

*in* (inn) by

*Gb* (geb) Geb, the earth god

*nb* (neb) every, any, all (cf. Lesson 4)

*ḥn'* (hena) together with

*psḏt* (pes-jet) Ennead or group of 9 gods

*pt* (pet) sky, heaven

*sḥtp* (sehetep) to pacify

*pr* (per) house

*nỉwt* (newt) town, city

*sḫr* (secher) plan, counsel

*ḫt* (chet) thing

*pn* (pen) this m(asculine) follows its noun (cf. Lesson 4)

*tn* (ten) this f(eminine) follows its noun (cf. Lesson 4)

*ky* (key) other, another m. precedes its noun (cf. Lesson 4)

*kt* (ket) other, another f. precedes its noun (cf. Lesson 4)

## EXERCISE 1

1. Learn and write out from memory the letters of the Egyptian alphabet.

2. Learn and write out from memory the words in Vocabulary 1.

   N.B.  The above exercises should be written in both hieroglyphs and transliteration.
   The transliteration will help the beginner to memorise the hieroglyphs. Now,

and at all stages, the hieroglyphs should be written with care, and the motto 'practice makes perfect' borne in mind ! The best results in writing hieroglyphs can be obtained if a drawing pen such as the Rotring 'Rapidograph', size 0.3, is used.

3. Write in hieroglyphs the following combinations of letters :

*3tp, ꭓ33t, 't, wbn, ptpt, mdt, nbyt, rwd*
Try to group the letters in the way that an Egyptian scribe might have done, with no ugly gaps between them.

## LESSON 2

### Ideograms and phonograms

There were two classes of signs in Egyptian hieroglyphic writing: ideograms and phonograms.

*Ideograms* are sense-signs; that is, they represent either the object depicted or some closely related idea. For instance, ⊙ not only means 'sun' but also 'day' or 'daytime' or 'daylight'. When the ideogram stands for the actual object depicted, it is usually followed by a stroke: e.g. ♀ *r'* 'sun'; ⚇ ı *ḥr* 'face'.

*Phonograms* are sound-signs; that is, they give the sound value associated with a sign. The sign may originally have been an ideogram; eventually it ceased to be used solely to denote an object and, by the rebus principle explained on page 37 came to represent objects or ideas which chanced to have a sound similar to that of the original sign. For example, the ideogram ▽ means 'mouth' and is transliterated *r*. *r* is also the preposition meaning 'towards' and can therefore be written by what is now the phonogram ⬯ .

*There are three kinds of phonogram:*

1. Those which represent single consonants and are called *uniliteral* signs e.g. the signs of the alphabet.
2. Those which represent a combination of two consonants and are called *biliteral* signs e.g. ᕊ =*m +n* (usually written *mn*) ;
          ⊏⊐ =*p +r* (*pr*).
3. Those which represent a combination of three consonants and are called *triliteral* signs e.g. ☥ =*n +f +r* (*nfr*) ;
          ⬭ =*ḥ +t +p* (*ḥtp*).

Biliteral and triliteral signs were used in much the same way as symbols such as & @ % £ are used in modern languages, that is, they are a convenient way of enlarging the alphabet by means of shorthand.

## Phonetic complements

Sometimes a biliteral or triliteral sign has two or more sound values. The Egyptians introduced the system of *phonetic complements* in order to indicate which sound was to be read. For example, the triliteral sign ☐ *ḥtp* was made easier to read by the addition of the two uniliteral signs ◠ ☐ (*t* + *p*), giving the group ☐. The reading of this group is still *ḥtp* (not *ḥtptp*) ; the last two signs are there simply to help the reader decide on the way in which the sign ☐ is to be read. Similarly, the biliteral sign ⊔⊔⊔ is read *mn*; in texts it is usually written ⬚. However, it is still read *mn* (not *mnn*) ; the final *n* confirms that the reading of the biliteral sign is *mn*.

At the beginning of each of the following lessons, examples of biliteral and triliteral signs will be given. If possible, they should be learned.

## Determinatives

The Egyptian scribes were faced with the problem of making clear the exact meaning of their written words. All languages have words which are homophones, that is, words which sound the same but have different meanings—the words 'wear' and 'were'; 'flour' and 'flower' in English, for example. The problem was made more difficult in Egyptian because the vowel sounds were not written. Thus, although many words may have been pronounced differently when spoken, they have the same appearance as each other when written. The confusion this could lead to will be appreciated if the following English words are read *ignoring the vowels*: leap, lop, alp, elope, lip, lap; slope, slip, slap, sleep, asleep; flop, flip, flap. It can be seen that a string of consonants can be very much modified as to reading and meaning by the addition of one or more vowels!

The Egyptians solved the problem by using ideograms. For example, 𓄂𓏤 $ḥs$ can mean 'to freeze' or 'to turn back'. In the spoken language, the word may have been pronounced differently according to meaning; in the written language, the only way the Egyptians had of distinguishing one meaning from the other was by using an ideogram (an idea-o-gram) at the end of the word to make the meaning clear. Thus, the ideogram 𓊝 (a sail) placed after $ḥs$ gives 𓄂𓊝, which means 'to freeze', the sail being used to indicate a (cold) wind. The ideogram 𓂻 (walking legs) placed after $ḥs$ gives 𓄂𓂻, which means 'turn back'.

When used in this way, ideograms are called '*determinatives*' because they determine the meaning of the signs written before them. For example, the word 𓊚 $šsp$ has at least four meanings; by using determinatives, the scribe could differentiate between them:

𓊚𓂝 $=šsp$ 'accept'

𓊚 $=šsp$ 'palm' (a unit of length)

𓊚 $=šsp$ 'statue'

𓊚 $=šsp$ 'daylight'.

Determinatives are used with almost every word. A word indicating that someone is walking, running, marching is often followed by the determinative 𓂻 , which is a sign representing legs. In order to illustrate an intangible idea, a product of the mind, the sign 𓏛 , which represents a rolled-up papyrus, is used. Thus determinatives can be used with abstract ideas as well as concrete objects.

Ideograms which act as determinatives to a number of different words cannot express the specific meaning of those words, but only the *kind* of sense borne by them. They are therefore called *generic determinatives*.

Determinatives were added to phonetic signs to indicate what the word represented. They have a *visual* value only; they are *not pronounced*.

Determinatives also serve another useful purpose. There were no gaps between words in written Egyptian, the signs followed on from each other in one unbroken sequence. Since determinatives only came at the ends of words, they can serve to aid the reader in breaking up the hieroglyphic signs into separate words.

There were over 100 generic determinatives in Egyptian; here is a list of some of the more important, which should be studied carefully so that the meanings indicated by the signs become familiar:

| Hieroglyph | Illustrates | Used as determinative to indicate |
|---|---|---|
| | seated man | men, men's names |
| | man with hand to mouth | eat, drink, speak, think |
| | man with basket on head | carry, lift, load |
| | man with sword | enemy, death |
| | man with stick | strength, action |
| | man with arms raised | praise, adore, greet |
| | young child | child, youth |

| Hieroglyph | Illustrates | Used as determinative to indicate |
|---|---|---|
| | seated woman | women, women's names |
| | seated man and woman | people |
| | seated god (note straight wig, curved beard) | god, king |
| | seated king (note coif, straight beard, uraeus on brow) | king |
| | king with flagellum | king |
| | king on stool | revered person, dead |
| | man leaning on staff | old, lean upon |
| | man with staff | official |
| | eye | see, sight |
| | ear of ox? | ear, hear |
| | nose, eye and cheek | nose, breath, joy |

| Hieroglyph | Illustrates | Used as determinative to indicate |
|---|---|---|
| | arms embracing | embrace, hold |
| | legs walking | go, come, enter |
| | legs walking backwards | retreat, withdraw |
| | leg | movement |
| | bull | cattle |
| | cow's skin | skin, animal |
| | piece of flesh | limbs, flesh |
| | pintail duck flying | fly |
| | swallow (note swallow tail) | great |
| | sparrow (note rounded tail) | bad, small |
| | cobra | goddess, especially those who took the form of cobra, e.g. Edjo, the Uraeus Goddess of Lower Egypt |

| *Hieroglyph* | *Illustrates* | *Used as determinative to indicate* |
|---|---|---|
| | herb | plant, flower |
| | branch | tree, wood |
| | sky | sky, heaven, above |
| | sun | sun, light, time |
| | sunshine | rays, shine |
| | sky with star suspended from it | night, dark |
| | flaming brazier | fire, heat, cook |
| | three ripples of water | water |
| | tongue of land | land, field, earth, river bank |
| | road bordered by shrubs | road, travel |
| | hill country | desert, foreign land |

| Hieroglyph | Illustrates | Used as determinative to indicate |
|---|---|---|
| ) | throw-stick | foreign, foreigner |
| ⌐⌐ | house | house, building |
| boat | boat on water | boat, navigate, sail north (Nile flows south to north), downstream, with flow of river |
| ship | ship under sail | sail south, upstream, against flow of river therefore sail used |
| ∏ | cloth on pole, emblem of divinity | god |
| knife | knife | knife, cut |
| hoe | hoe | cultivate, hack up |
| X | two sticks crossed | break, divide, reckon |
| jug | beer jug | pot, vessel, anoint, liquid |

A comprehensive list of hieroglyphic signs can be found in Gardiner's 'Egyptian Grammar', pp. 438-548.

## ulary to Lesson 2

(ray) sun

(her) face

o) mouth

*ḥs* (hes) to freeze ; with determinative ⌒ , to turn back (ḥsỉ)

*šsp* (shesep) to accept, receive

palm

statue

daylight

*nfr* (nefer) good, beautiful,
happy (cf. Lesson 4)

*t* (tar) bread (also written ⊖ )

*ḥnḳt* (henket) beer (also written ⊖ )

*rnpt* (renpet) year

*drt* (deret) hand (varr.
*ḏrt* (djeret) )

*mnt* (ment) thigh

*spt* (sepet) lip

*ḥf3w* (hefaroo) snake

## EXERCISE 2

1. Practise writing hieroglyphs by writing out the determinatives from the list given above.

2. Write in hieroglyphs the following combinations of letters, remembering to take care to group them according to Egyptian usage !
   h3w, h3t, ḥb, ḥt, ḫt, sbḳ, šbw, ḳbḥ, k3, gr, tỉtỉ, twt, ṯsm, dn, ḏt

F

## LESSON 3

### Some common biliteral signs

| | | | | | | | |
|---|---|---|---|---|---|---|---|
| 𓄿 | 3w | 𓐝 | 3b, mr | 𓄿 | 3ḫ | 𓅑 | iw |
| 𓍋 | im, gs | 𓏶 | im | 𓇋 | in | 𓁹 | ir |
| 𓇋 | is | 𓂝, 𓊬 | '3 | 𓅱 | 'ḳ | 𓂧 | 'ḏ |

### Some common triliteral signs

| | | | | | | | | | |
|---|---|---|---|---|---|---|---|---|---|
| 𓉼 | iwn | 𓎛 | 'wt | 𓋹 | 'nḫ | 𓂭 | 'ḥ3 | 𓎺 | 'ḥ' |

### Nouns

In English, a noun is the *name* of something. For example, in the sentence 'the teacher sent the naughty girl to be punished by the headmaster', the words 'teacher', 'girl' and 'headmaster' are *nouns*. The words 'angry' and 'naughty' are *adjectives*, that is, they are words which *describe* a noun.

In English, adjectives do not change their form; 'naughty' would still be written in the same way if it had been used to describe a boy and not a girl, or if it had been used to describe several girls. In many languages, however, adjectives do change their form, according to the *gender* of the noun they are describing. If an adjective is being used to describe a masculine noun it is written in a different way from one used to describe a feminine noun. In both cases it is possible to find a third way of writing the adjective if it is being used to describe a plural noun.

## Gender

Egyptian nouns have two genders, *feminine* and *masculine*. Most feminine nouns end in *t* e.g. 🝰 *st* 'woman', 🝰 *nĩwt* 'town'. Nouns which do not end in *t* are usually masculine e.g. 🝰 *r'* 'sun', 🝰 *ḥr* 'face'. The sense of the English *neuter* (it, thing) is expressed in Egyptian by the feminine e.g. 🝰 *dwt* 'evil thing'.

## Definite and indefinite article

In Middle Egyptian the article, whether definite (the) or indefinite (a, an) is not normally written. Thus, 🝰 *rn* may be translated as 'the name', 'a name' or 'name' according to context.

## Writing the plural

In English, nouns denoting one thing are *singular*, whilst those denoting more than one thing are *plural*. The plural is usually formed simply by adding an s to the singular, as: book, books; or by changing the last letter(s) of the noun before adding an s, as: fly, flies; wife, wives. Some nouns change completely from singular to plural, as: man, men; foot, feet.

There are two ways of indicating the plural in Egyptian:

1. the singular form can be written out three times:

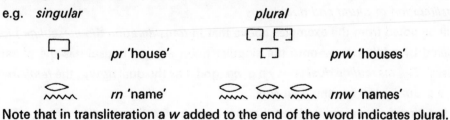

e.g.   *singular*                                   *plural*

🝰 *pr* 'house'                          🝰 *prw* 'houses'

🝰 *rn* 'name'                          🝰 *rnw* 'names'

Note that in transliteration a *w* added to the end of the word indicates plural.

2. a determinative consisting of three strokes which can be written ׀׀׀ ; ׀ ׀ ׀ or ׀ ׀
according to artistic preference, can be used:

e.g.  *singular*                                            *plural*

     *nṯr* 'god'                          *nṯrw* 'gods'

     *pr* 'house'                         *prw* 'houses'.

## The dual form

If the Egyptian scribe wished to indicate *pairs* of things or persons he used what we call
the *dual form* which is indicated by writing out the singular noun twice instead of three
times as in the plural. Sometimes, the sign       is used to indicate the dual; in this case,
the       is added to the singular form of the noun and the determinative is written twice.
This second method is most often used with words which are commonly written with
several hieroglyphic signs:

e.g.  *singular*                                            *dual*

     *pr* 'house'                         *prwy* 'two houses'

     *ỉrt* 'eye'                          *ỉrty* 'two eyes'

     *nṯr* 'god'                          *nṯrwy* 'pair of gods'

     *snt* 'sister'                       *snty* 'two sisters'

## Transliteration of plural and dual forms

It will be noted from the examples above that in *transliteration* the *masculine plural* is
rendered by adding a *-w* onto the singular noun e.g. *pr* 'house' has the plural *prw*
'houses'. The *masculine dual* is *-wy* e.g. *nṯr* 'god' has the dual *nṯrwy*; the *feminine dual*
is *-y* e.g. *snt* 'sister' has the dual *snty*.

It has already been pointed out that the *singular feminine* ending is *t* e.g.       *st*

'woman'. In transliteration, the *plural feminine* ending is *-wt* e.g. ⌐𓏏𓆸⌐ *swt* 'women'.
   The Egyptian scribe often omitted to write out plural and dual endings.


## Numbers

*The writing of numerals*

A vertical stroke | is used when writing the numbers 1-9; special signs are used to write the multiples of ten. The seven signs employed are:

| 1 | \| | (*w'*) | 10,000 | 𓂭 | (*ḏb'*) |
|---|---|---|---|---|---|
| 10 | ∩ | (*mḏ*) | 100,000 | 𓆐 | (*ḥfn*) |
| 100 | 𓏤 | (*št*) | 1,000,000 | 𓁨 | (*ḥḥ*) |
| 1,000 | 𓆼 | (*ḥ3*) | | | |

The higher values are written in front of the lower. If an Egyptian scribe wished to write the number 1,245, he would start with the highest value sign (𓆼 —1,000) then the next highest (𓏤 —100, writing the sign twice to indicate 200); then the tens and the units, each being written out as many times as necessary to indicate the total—four times in the case of the tens, five for the units; thus he would write 1,245 as 𓆼𓏤𓏤∩∩∩|||||.

e.g.  𓆼𓏤𓏤 ||| |||  1,208

   𓏤𓏤𓏤 ∩∩ |||
   𓏤𓏤  ∩∩ |||   546

   \|\|\|  ∩∩   30,030


## Cardinal numbers

1. The numeral *follows* the noun; the noun is usually in the singular form:

e.g.   🐦 ‖   *s* 2   '2 men'

   🐟 ∩   *mḥ* 10   '10 cubits'.

2. The words for 1,000 and 1,000,000 are sometimes written *before* their noun, which is written in the singular, and are connected to it by 🐦 *m* (being) or 〜〜 *n* (of):

   e.g.   ꗏ   *ḫ3 m t ḥnkt* 'a thousand of bread and beer' (lit: a thousand being bread and beer)

   ꗏ 〜〜 ∫∫∫   *ḫ3 n rnpwt* 'a thousand years' (lit: a thousand of years).

## Vocabulary to Lesson 3

𓊃 *st* woman

𓇳 *r'* sun

𓑇 *ḏwt* evil, sadness

𓂋𓈖 *rn* name

𓊹 *nṯr* god

𓁹 *irt* eye

𓊃𓈖𓏏 *snt* sister

𓀀 *s* man

𓄠 *mḥ* cubit

𓈐 *w3t* way, road, side

𓂋 *ds* jug

𓂧𓏠 *dmi* town

□ var. 𓎟 *nb* lord, master

⊻ varr. ⊻ , ⟷ *t3* earth, land

⊻ *t3wy* the Two Lands i.e. Egypt

𓇓 var. 𓇓〜〜 *nsw* king, king of Upper Egypt

⟶ var. 𓊖 *Kmt* the Black Land i.e. Egypt

𓇳 var. 𓇳 *nḥḥ* eternity

𓅨 varr. 𓅨 , 𓅨 *wr* prince, great one

𓄿 *ḥmt* woman, wife

𓅭 *s3t* daughter

𓇓 *šrr* small

later 𓇓 *šri* small

## EXERCISE 3

(a) *Write in hieroglyphs and transliteration*

   1. two hands   2. two thighs   3. two lips
   4. twenty years   5. seventy-five snakes   6. a thousand towns.

Paased Ra          2yrs ago?

(b) *Translate into English*

1.  🦅𓂝𓃀 𓏤 | |

2.  𓊪𓊪𓊪 𓈖𓈖𓈖 | | | ～～～ 𓆑 𓂓

3.  𓆑 𓇋 𓈖𓈖𓈖

4.  𓊪 𓏺

5.  𓇋𓂝𓍯𓂋𓊪 𓂋𓏤

# LESSON 4

## More biliteral signs

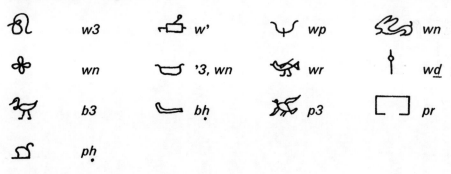

| | | | | | | | |
|---|---|---|---|---|---|---|---|
| | *w3* | | *w'* | | *wp* | | *wn* |
| | *wn* | | *'3, wn* | | *wr* | | *w<u>d</u>* |
| | *b3* | | *b<u>h</u>* | | *p3* | | *pr* |
| | *p<u>h</u>* | | | | | | |

## More triliteral signs

| | | | | | | | |
|---|---|---|---|---|---|---|---|
| | *w3<u>h</u>* | | *w'b* | | *w3s, <u>d</u>'m* | | *<u>d</u>3m* |

## The genitive

In English, the genitive is expressed by the word 'of' e.g. 'the knave *of* hearts', 'the Queen *of* the May'.

There are two ways of expressing the genitive in Egyptian: one in which the 'of' is written, the other in which it is not. The former is called the *indirect genitive*, the latter is called the *direct genitive*.

1. *The direct genitive* is formed by placing two nouns next to each other with no intervening word, as if in English we were to express the phrase 'Lord of the Two

Lands' as 'Lord the Two Lands' e.g. ▽ 🏺 *nb t3wy* 'Lord (of) the Two Lands'. The direct genitive is used when the connection between the two nouns is particularly close, although this is not an absolute rule.

2. *The indirect genitive* uses the so-called *genitival adjective* 〰️ *ny* by interposing it between the two nouns e.g. 'the King of Egypt' 𓇓𓏏𓈖 𓆓 〰️ 𓎟 𓊪𓏤 *nsw ny Kmt.*

The genitival adjective changes according to whether the noun which goes before it is masculine, feminine or plural.

If the preceding noun is *masculine*, the genitive is written 〰️ *ny*, as in 'the King of Egypt'—*nsw ny Kmt*—above.

If the preceding noun is *feminine*, the genitive is written 〰️ *nyt* e.g 𓊪𓏤 〰️ 𓇋𓇋𓇋 ⊙ *nỉwt nyt nḥḥ* 'the city of eternity'.

If the preceding noun is *plural*, the genitive is written 𓏤 *nyw* when the noun is masculine, or 〰️ *nywt* when the noun is feminine e.g. 𓅨𓅆 𓆓 𓏤 𓊪𓏤 *wrw nyw nỉwt* 'the great ones of the city'; 𓊪 𓆓 〰️ 𓏤 *ḥmwt nywt wrw* 'the wives of the chiefs'.

The *transliterations* given above of the genitival adjective are somewhat pedantic. It is more usual to transliterate the masculine singular as *n*, not as *ny*; the feminine singular as *nt*, not *nyt*; and the plural, both masculine and feminine, as *nw*, not as *nyw* and *nywt*.

Generally speaking, the indirect genitive is more commonly used than the direct.

## Adjectives

In Egyptian, adjectives *follow* the nouns which they are describing, and *agree with them in number and gender* (see pages 75-76 for writings of feminine and plural) :

e.g. 𓇋𓏤𓎛𓂋𓀀𓏤 *sḫr pn bìn* 'this evil counsel' (lit: counsel this evil)

𓎟𓏏 *ḫt nbt nfrt* 'every good thing' (lit: thing every good)

*s3t šrìt* 'the little daughter' (lit: daughter little)

An exception to the rule that adjectives follow their nouns is *ky* (m.), *kt* (f.) 'other', 'another', which *precedes* its noun:

e.g. *ky rn* 'another name'

*kt ḫt* 'another thing'.

Adjectives can be used to form nouns. In this case they usually have an appropriate determinative.

e.g. *šrì* 'small boy' i.e. adjective (small) plus the determinative

*nfrt* 'beautiful woman' i.e. adjective (beautiful) plus feminine ending plus determinative

*nfrt* 'fine cow' i.e. adjective plus feminine ending plus determinative.

## Vocabulary to Lesson 4

| | |
|---|---|
| *ḥm* male servant | varr. , *ìmy-r* overseer |
| *ḥmt* female servant | *ìnw* produce |
| var. *ḥm* Majesty | *sḫt* country |
| *wbn* to shine | *mw* water |
| *hrw* day, daytime | *ìt* father |
| *mnḫ* (be) efficient | *b3kt* handmaiden |
| *sḫty* fowler, peasant | *ḥnwt* mistress |
| | var. *ḥm-nṯr* priest |

**EXERCISE 4**

(a) *Write in hieroglyphs and transliteration*
1. This beautiful house.
2. This beautiful woman.
3. The wife of the priest.
4. The house of the master.
5. An efficient overseer of the city.

(b) *Translate into English*

1.

2.

3.

4.

5.

# LESSON 5

## More biliteral signs

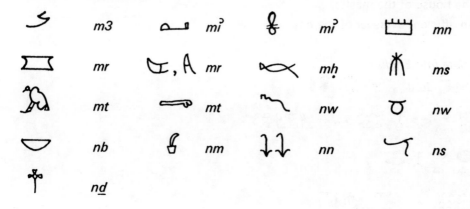

| | | | | | | | |
|---|---|---|---|---|---|---|---|
| | *m3* | | *mi* | | *mi* | | *mn* |
| | *mr* | | *mr* | | *mḥ* | | *ms* |
| | *mt* | | *mt* | | *nw* | | *nw* |
| | *nb* | | *nm* | | *nn* | | *ns* |
| | *nḏ* | | | | | | |

## More triliteral signs

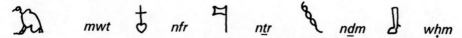

| | | | | | | | |
|---|---|---|---|---|---|---|---|
| | *mwt* | | *nfr* | | *nṯr* | | *nḏm* | | *wḥm* |

## Prepositions

In English, a *preposition* is a word which shows the relationship between a noun or pronoun and some other word in a sentence. For example, in the phrases 'the book is *in* my hand', 'the book is *beside* my hand', 'the book is *under* my hand', the words 'in', 'beside' and 'under' are all prepositions.

The chief prepositions in Egyptian are:

1. 𓅓 *m* (before suffix-pronouns (see page 92) written 𓇋𓅓 *ỉm*) *in, from with*
   (i) 'in' a place e.g. in the house
   (ii) 'in' time e.g. in summer, for three years
   (iii) 'from' a place e.g. I went out from the house
   (iv) 'with' an instrument e.g. with my strong arm

2. 𓂋 *r to, towards; against*
   (i) 'to' a place e.g. to heaven, to the city, towards the house
   (ii) 'against' somebody e.g. I took action against my enemy

3. 𓈖 *n to* a person (i.e. the dative) e.g. I speak to the boy, I gave it to my mother

4. 𓁷 *ḥr upon, because* (𓁶 before suffix-pronouns)
   (i) 'upon' a place e.g. upon the water, on my feet
   (ii) cause e.g. pleased with (because of) something; on account of; sad concerning (because of) someone; about

5. 𓇋𓈖 *ỉn by* e.g. for recitation by Geb

6. 𓐍𓏏 *ḫft in front of* e.g. before your face

7. 𓏇 *mỉ like* e.g. like a dream

8. 𓎛𓈖 *ḥn' together with* e.g. with his Ennead

9. 𓅓𓃀𓎛 *m-b3ḥ in the presence of, before* e.g. before the king

10. 𓅓𓐍𓏏 *m-ḫt after* e.g. after death, after he died

## Adverbs

Adverbs are words whose main function is to describe verbs; they can also describe any part of speech except a noun or a pronoun. For example, in the following sentences: 'the boy came early'; 'the bird sang sweetly'; 'he works hard'; 'the river flows fast', the words early, sweetly, hard and fast are adverbs.

Sometimes, an adverb is expanded into a phrase, thus forming the so-called 'adverbial phrase'. For example, in the sentence 'we rise early', 'early' is an adverb describing the verb 'rise'. If 'early' were to be expanded into a phrase, it could become 'we rise *at six o'clock in the morning*'. Adverbial phrases can be made up of a preposition plus a noun e.g. 'the cows were sold *in the market*'. Further examples of adverbial phrases are 'they met him *on his arrival*'; 'he waited *until 4 o'clock*'.

Egyptian has very few true adverbs. It makes up for the lack by using *adverbial phrases* which are *formed by placing a preposition before a noun* (see English examples above).

e.g. the sun rises *in the sky*    𓅱𓃀𓈖 𓇳 𓂋 𓅓 𓊪𓏏    *wbn rꜤ m pt*

he went *into the city on this day* 𓉐𓂋𓂋𓆑 𓊖 𓅓 𓉔𓂋𓅱𓇳 𓊪𓈖    *pr.f r*

*nꜣiwt m hrw pn*

(the words *underlined* are adverbial phrases).

## Vocabulary to Lesson 5

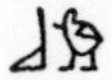

𓃀𓏤 *bw* place

𓇳𓏤𓁦 *RꜤ* Re, the sun god

𓅨𓏤 *wr* great (adj.)

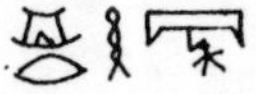

𓎼𓂋𓎛 *grḥ* night

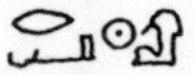

𓉔𓂋𓅱𓇳 *hrw* day

𓂋𓍑𓂋𓅱 *r-ḏrw* to the limits of

𓄡𓏏 *ẖt* body, belly

𓉺𓈖𓈖 � *iwnn* sanctuary

𓊹𓏤 𓏤𓏤𓏤𓏤 *sḫnt* four supports of heaven

𓆓𓂧 *ḏd* to say, to tell

𓄔𓂋𓅓 *sḏm* to hear, to obey

𓉔𓐠𓂧 *h3b* to send

𓂋𓂧 var. 𓂝 , 𓂝𓏤 *rdí* or *dí* to give, to place

**EXERCISE 5**

(a) *Write in hieroglyphs and transliteration*
  1. To another place.
  2. To Geb, together with Re.
  3. In this great name.
  4. In all lands.
  5. In the presence of Ptah.

(b) *Translate into English*

  1. [hieroglyphs]

  2. [hieroglyphs]

  3. [hieroglyphs]

  4. [hieroglyphs]

# LESSON 6

One of the things that the reader will notice about Ancient Egyptian inscriptions, whether they be short or long, on the walls or columns of temples, on the walls of tombs, on the lids of coffins, on decorative bands on furniture, or on statue bases, is that in many of them one or more *cartouches* stand out.

We have already seen that Champollion used cartouches as the starting point from which he was able to decipher hieroglyphs. So, too, can the reader use them for his first attempts to read 'real' hieroglyphs as opposed to those in the Exercises he may have been attempting as he reads through this book.

From the latter part of the Old Kingdom onwards, each king of Egypt adopted a royal titulary on his accession to the throne; this titulary consisted of five names. From Dynasty V onwards, the last two were put inside cartouches when they were written in inscriptions. The cartouche names were: 'the King of Upper and Lower Egypt ( $\frac{1}{4}$ ⳡ *nsw bỉt*) ⬭⬭⬭⬭ ; 'the Son of Re ( ⳡ☉ *s3 R'*) ⬭⬭⬭⬭ . The former is the religious name of the king, adopted on his succession to the throne, the latter is the name borne by the king before his accession and is almost equivalent to a family name.

The most desirable way to practise reading cartouches is, of course, to go to Egypt and find them on the monuments there! As this is not practicable for everyone, a visit to the nearest museum, which will probably have at least some Egyptian objects in its collection, will have to suffice.

In order to help the reader when he first comes into contact with cartouches, the following examples are given for him to attempt to translate. All the words used in the following cartouches will be found in the Egyptian-English Vocabulary on page 137. As usual the answers will be found in the Key to Exercises.

## EXERCISE 6

### Hints before starting

Modern interpretations of the ways in which kings' names are transliterated, and pronounced, vary, due mainly to the lack of written vowels in Egyptian. Several versions will be found in books of Egyptology; in fact, the form of royal name used is more often than not the Greek rather than the Egyptian.

In cartouches where an element of the king's name is the name of a god, then the god's name was written first out of reverence even though it might be pronounced last. e.g. the name of the Dynasty IV king, Mycerinus, is written ⊙ ⎵ 𝖴𝖴𝖴 ; *R'* ( ⊙ ) *mn* ( ⎵ ) *k3w* ( 𝖴 𝖴 𝖴 ) with the name of the sun god, Re, written first. It is, however, read *mn-k3w-R'*—abiding (*mn*) are the spirits (*k3w*) of Re (*R'*). Mycerinus is the Greek form of *mn-k3w-R'*.

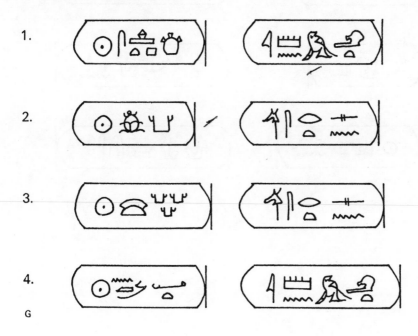

G

5.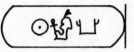

6.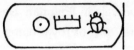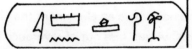

7.

8.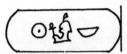

9.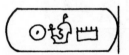

10.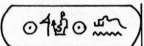

## LESSON 7

### More biliteral signs

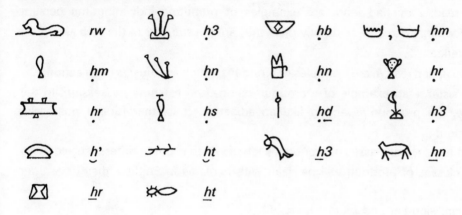

### More triliteral signs

### Pronouns

In English, a pronoun is a word that stands in place of a noun. Without pronouns, English sentences would be very clumsy. For instance:

'Robert went to the shelf. Robert picked up a book. Robert read the book. Then Robert gave the book to Robert's sister. Robert and Robert's sister liked the book when Robert and Robert's sister had read the book.'

When the above paragraph is rewritten using, where necessary, pronouns in place of nouns, a more satisfactory version is obtained:

'Robert went to the shelf and picked up a book. He read the book and then gave it to his sister. Both Robert and his sister liked the book when they had read it.'

The words underlined in the above paragraph are pronouns: he, it, his, they. They demonstrate between them three different ways of using pronouns:

(i) *He* read, *they* had read, are examples of pronouns indicating the persons *performing an action*. In other words, they are the *subjects* of the verb and of the sentence.

(ii) Gave *it*, had read *it*, are examples of pronouns which are *objects* of an action.

(iii) *His* sister is an example of a pronoun being used to show *possession*. In this case, the pronoun is acting like an adjective. It is, therefore, a possessive pronoun.

Egyptian has several classes of pronoun, each of which is put to different use or uses. Only two classes of pronoun will be dealt with here; as in English, they have three *persons*:

1st person, singular and plural: I, we, etc.

2nd person, singular and plural: thou, you, etc.

3rd person, singular and plural: he, she, it, they, etc.

1. *Suffix-pronouns*, so called because they must *follow* and *be joined on to* (suffixed to) a preceding word:

| Singular | | Plural |
|---|---|---|
| .*ỉ* I, my, me | 1st person<br>m and f | .*n* we, our, us |
| .*k* thou, thy, thee<br>.*t* thou. thy, thee | 2nd person<br>m<br>f  / m and f | .*tn* you, your |
| .*f* he, his, its, him, it<br>.*s* she, her, its, it | 3rd person<br>m<br>f  / m and f | .*sn* they, their, them |

*Uses of the suffix-pronouns*

Suffix-pronouns have three main uses:

  (i) They are used to denote the person *performing an action*

    e.g. 〰 *ḏd.s* (verb *ḏd* +suffix 3rd person fem *s*) 'she says'

        *sḏm.i̓* (verb *sḏm* +suffix 1st person sing) 'I say'.

  (ii) They are used to show *possession*

    e.g. (noun *pr* +suffix 2nd person m) 'your house'

       (noun *snt* +suffix 3rd person m) 'his sister'.

  (iii) They are used *after prepositions*

    e.g. *n.i̓* 'to me'

        *ḥnʽ.sn* 'with them'.

2. *Dependent pronouns*, which are not as closely attached to a preceding word as the suffix-pronouns, can never stand as the first word of a sentence.

The dependent pronouns are written as follows:

| Singular | | Plural |
|---|---|---|
| *wi̓* I, me | 1st person m and f | *n* we, us |
| *ṯw* thou, thee<br>*ṯn* thou, thee | 2nd person m / f   m and f | *ṯn* you |
| *sw* he, him, it<br>*sy* she, her, it<br>*st* it | 3rd person m / f / n   m and f | *sn* they, them |

*Uses of the dependent pronouns*

The three main uses of the dependent pronouns are:

(i) To denote the object of an action

e.g. 𓂋𓀁 *h3b.k wi* (verb *h3b* +suffix 2nd person singular + dependent pronoun *wi* as object of verb) 'you send me';

*rdi.f st* (verb *rdi* +suffix 3rd person singular + dependent pronoun *st* as object of verb) 'he gives it'.

(ii) After certain particles such as 𓇋𓋴𓏏 *ist* 'lo'; � *mk* 'behold'

e.g. *mk wi m-b3ḥ.k* 'Behold I am before you' (lit: Behold me before you).

(iii) Reflexively

e.g. *rdi.i wi ḥr ḫt.i* 'I place myself on my belly'.


## Vocabulary to Lesson 7

*sš* scribe        *imnt* the West

*wbn* to rise (of sun)      var. *dw3t* the Underworld

*ršw* to rejoice      var. *sb3* door

*'imn* Amun, god      var. *dw* mountain

*m-ḥ3t* in front of      *3wt* oblations, gifts


## EXERCISE 7

(a) *Write in hieroglyphs and transliteration*

1. This thy beautiful house.
2. His beautiful wife.
3. In his house.
4. Their city.

(b) *Translate into English*

1. [hieroglyphs]

2. [hieroglyphs]

3. [hieroglyphs]

4. [hieroglyphs]

## LESSON 8

### More biliteral signs

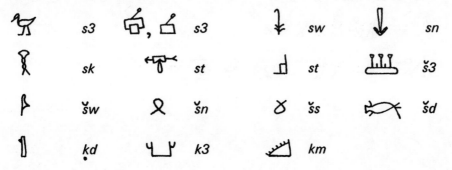

| | | | | | | | |
|---|---|---|---|---|---|---|---|
| 𓇉 | s3 | 𓋴, 𓋶 | s3 | 𓋪 | sw | 𓌡 | sn |
| 𓋴 | sk | 𓊃 | st | 𓊪 | st | 𓈙 | š3 |
| 𓆷 | šw | 𓏏 | šn | 𓐍 | šs | 𓆞 | šd |
| 𓎡 | ḳd | 𓎢 | k3 | 𓐝 | km | | |

### More triliteral signs

| | | | | | | | |
|---|---|---|---|---|---|---|---|
| � | sb3 |  𓄜 | sm3 |  𓄲 | sḥm |  𓅂 | tyw |

### Verbs

A verb is a word which tells us what somebody or something does. For example, in the passage 'The frog dived into the water and brought up the ball. With a joyful cry, the princess picked up the ball': the words 'dived', 'brought up' and 'picked up' are verbs. Schoolchildren are often taught that a verb is a doing word!

In English, the *tense* of a verb refers to the time in which an action takes place. There are three tenses—present, past and future, all, in English, clearly distinct from each other. For example, with the verb 'to arrive', the *present tense* is 'I arrive', the *past tense* is 'I arrived', the *future tense* is 'I shall arrive'.

In Egyptian, the distinctions between tenses are not so clearly marked. Take, for example, the sentence 𓅱𓈖𓇳 𓂋𓇳𓅓𓏏𓇯 *wbn r' m pt.* 𓅱𓈖𓇳 (*wbn*) is the verb 'to rise'; 𓂋𓇳 (*r'*) and 𓊪𓏏𓇯 (*pt*) are nouns meaning 'sun' and 'sky' respectively; 𓅓 (*m*) is the preposition 'in'. The sentence can be translated in the following ways:

'the sun rises in the sky' (verb in present tense)

'the sun rose in the sky' (verb in past tense)

'the sun will rise in the sky' (verb in future tense).

Only context will indicate the tense in which to put the verb in translation. Note, here, that in Egyptian the verb is placed at the beginning of the sentence (see further page 101).

Egyptian does have several verb-forms which can be used to clearly indicate past, future, continuous activity, tenses etc. Beginners, however, need not concern themselves with these verb-forms. Instead, we will concentrate on what may be called an 'all-purpose' tense, the *sḏm.f* (pronounced 'sedjemef') form of the verb.

## The *sḏm.f* form of the verb

If we analyse the sentence discussed above, *wbn r' m pt*, we find that the subject of the sentence, that is, the noun performing the action of the verb, is *r'* (sun). The verb is *wbn* (rise). In this instance, the *subject* of the sentence (*r'*) has been added on to the *stem of the verb* (*wbn*). This is how the Egyptians made up the *sḏm.f* form of the verb: they took the stem of a verb and added on to it the subject, which could be a noun or a suffix-pronoun.

When describing the various parts of the Egyptian verb, it is usual to take the stem of the verb 𓄔𓅓 *sḏm* 'to hear' as the model. If we add to it as subject the 3rd person masculine singular suffix-pronoun, *f*, the name of the verb form *sḏm.f* is obtained.

The paradigm, or model, of the *sḏm.f* form is as follows:

1st sing. m and f      𓄔𓅓𓀀      *sḏm.ỉ*      I hear

2nd sing. m            𓄔𓅓𓂝      *sḏm.k*      thou hearest

| | | | |
|---|---|---|---|
| 2nd sing. f | | *sḏm.t* | thou hearest |
| 3rd sing. m | | *sḏm.f* | he (or it) hears |
| 3rd sing. f | | *sḏm.s* | she (or it) hears |
| 1st plural m and f | | *sḏm.n* | we hear |
| 2nd plural m and f | | *sḏm.tn* | you hear |
| 3rd plural m and f | | *sḏm.sn* | they hear |

When the *subject* of the sḏm.f form is a *suffix-pronoun*, it must *never* be separated from the verb-stem. When, on the other hand, the subject is a *noun*, this can sometimes be separated from the verb-stem:

e.g.      *ḏd.s n.f* 'she says to him' *but*

     *ḏd n.f sš* 'the scribe says to him'.

## Uses of the sḏm.f form

1. The *sḏm.f* form can be used to express the *present tense* of a verb:
   e.g.    *wbn rʿ m pt* 'the sun rises in the sky'.
2. It can be used to express the *past tense*:
   e.g.    *h3b.k sš r nỉwt* 'you sent the scribe into the town'.
3. It can be used to express the *future tense*:
   e.g.    *rš s3t.ỉ* 'my daughter shall rejoice'.
4. It can be used to express a *wish* or a *command*:
   e.g.    *h3b.k sš* 'may you send the scribe' *or* 'send a scribe!'

The context in which the sentence containing the verb is found will determine the tense of the *sḏm.f* form.

## A note on transliteration

Some verbs end in the semi-vowels 𓇋 *i* or 𓅱 *w*, even though these letters may not actually be written out in hieroglyphs e.g. 𓉔𓄿𓂻 *h3i*; 𓂧𓄿𓂻 *ḏ3i*. When the *sḏm.f* form of many of these verbs is *transliterated*, the 𓇋 or the 𓅱 falls away. Thus 𓉐𓂻 *pri* becomes *pr.f* not *pri.f*; 𓂋𓈙𓅱 *ršw* becomes *rš.f* not *ršw.f*. All the verbs ending in 𓇋 or 𓅱 used in this Grammar display this tendency with the exception of 𓂋𓂞 *rdi*, which is transliterated *rdi.f*.

## Vocabulary to Lesson 8

𓂋 *r* utterance

�мардd𓊛 *dpt* boat

𓉔𓄿𓂻 *h3i* to go down

𓅱𓇋𓄿 *wi3* sacred barque

� *ḥdi* to fare downstream

𓉐𓇋 *h'i* to appear, to shine

𓈍𓏏 *3ḫt* horizon

𓂧𓏏 *ḏt* eternity

𓂧𓄿𓂻 *ḏ3i* to cross

𓌳𓄿𓄿 *m33* to see

𓅬𓅓𓄿 *gmi* to find

� *ḥḳr* hungry man

𓏶𓈗 *ini* to bring, to remove

𓈙𓃀𓅱 *šbw* food

## EXERCISE 8

(a) *Write in hieroglyphs and transliteration*

   1. Tell your name to the scribe.

   2. You shall say to your son.

3. He rejoices because of her utterances.
4. The scribe sent this boat.
5. He shall fare downstream to the city, his daughter with him.

**(b)** *Translate into English*

1. [hieroglyphs]

2. [hieroglyphs]

3. [hieroglyphs]

4. [hieroglyphs]

# LESSON 9

## More biliteral signs

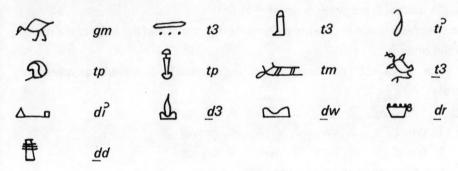

| | | | | | | | |
|---|---|---|---|---|---|---|---|
| | gm | | t3 | | t3 | | ti' |
| | tp | | tp | | tm | | t3 |
| | di' | | d3 | | dw | | dr |
| | dd | | | | | | |

## More triliteral signs

| | | | | | |
|---|---|---|---|---|---|
| | db3 | | db' | | dsr |

## Sentences and clauses

*Word order in sentences*

The normal word order in Egyptian sentences is:

1. verb  2. subject (noun or suffix-pronoun)  3. object (noun)  4. adverb or adverbial phrase (preposition + noun):

e.g.

    1. *m3*    2. *s*    3. *sš*    4. *m niwt*

    1. saw    2. man    3. scribe    4. in city

    (i.e. the man saw the scribe in the city) ;

*or*

1. 🦅📿  2. 〰  3. 𓊹 |  4. 🌱 ⛉
1. *gm*        2. *.f*      3. *s*      4. *ḥr wȝt*
1. found   w. he   3. man   4. on road

(i.e. he found the man on the road).

Sometimes, the *normal word order is upset*:

   (i)  when the *object* is not a noun but a *dependent pronoun* and the *subject* is a noun, then the order is:

   1. verb  2. object (pronoun)  3. subject (noun)  4. adverb or **adverbial phrase**:

   e.g. 1. 🦅📿  2. ⚡ℓ  3. 𓊹 |  4. 🌱 ⛉
   1. *gm*       2. *sw*      3. *s*      4. *ḥr wȝt*
   1. found   2. him   3. man   4. on road

   (i.e. the man found him on the road);

   (ii)  when the *dative* ** is used, then the word order is:

   1. verb  2. subject  3. object  4. dative  5. adverb or adverbial phrase:

   e.g. 1. △◿  2. 𓊹 |  3. ⌐⌐  4. 〰 𓏤𓊹¦  5. 📿⊗ 〰
   1. *dỉ*    2. *s*      3. *tȝ*    4. *n ḥkrw*       5. *m nỉwt.f*
   1. gives  2. man  3. bread  4. to hungry   5. in his city

   (i.e. the man gives bread to the hungry in his city);

   (iii)  when the dative is used, not with a noun but with a *pronoun*, the rule is that *a noun must not precede a pronoun*; and that *the dependent pronoun must not precede a suffix-pronoun*:

   e.g. 𓉔🦅🏺〰▦✚𓊹 𓊹|     *hȝb   n.k   sš   s*
                                                sends  to you  scribe  man
                                                (i.e. the scribe sends the man to you);

   🏠〰|◻▦✚𓊹     *ỉn      n.k     st sš*
                                     brings  to you  it  scribe
                                     (i.e. the scribe brings it to you).

✗ the man who is a scribe?

**In Egyptian, the dative is formed by placing the preposition ~~~ *n* (see page 84) before a noun or a suffix-pronoun. In the sentences 'I gave money to the man' and 'I gave the money to him' the phrases underlined are datives.

## Clauses

If two sentences such as 'the girl was intelligent' and 'the girl was good' are joined together by the conjunction 'and', they are called *clauses*. As each clause in itself makes complete sense, they are said to be *independent* of each other.

Clauses that are connected by conjunctions such as 'after', 'when', 'if', 'though', 'for' are not always independent. For example, in the sentence 'the man was paid after the work had been done', the clause 'the man was paid' can by itself make complete sense, and is therefore an *independent clause*. The clause 'after the work had been done', however, does not make complete sense on its own; it depends upon the first clause in order to make sense. It is called, therefore, a *dependent clause*.

In Egyptian, conjunctions are hardly ever used to indicate dependent clauses. The translator is left to decide for himself the logical connection between clauses. Thus the sentence ⟨glyphs⟩ *wbn r' m pt* which was translated in previous Lessons as an independent clause meaning 'the sun rises in the sky' can also be translated as a dependent clause meaning:

> when the sun rises in the sky
> if the sun rises in the sky
> so that the sun might rise in the sky
> after the sun had risen in the sky etc.,

according to context.

## Vocabulary to Lesson 9

| | | | |
|---|---|---|---|
| rḫ to know | | s3 back | |
| dd to tell n to someone | | iri to do, to act, to make | |
| ỉb heart, wish (noun) | | ḥ3t front | |
| ỉbỉ to be thirsty | | ḥ3ty-' local prince | |
| ỉbt thirst | | pri to go out | |
| š't despatch | | ḫrw voice, cry | |
| '3 donkey | | wts to wear, to lift up, to carry | |
| dšrt the Red Land i.e. the desert | | ḥdt the White Crown (of Upper Egypt) | |
| dšrt the Red Crown (of Lower Egypt) | | | |

## EXERCISE 9

(a) *Write in hieroglyphs and transliteration*

1. The scribe knows a plan on this day.
2. Your lord has sent to us every good thing.
3. The woman found him upon the road.
4. She gave him bread and beer.
5. He told us his wish.

(b) *Translate into English*

1. 

2. 

3.

## LESSON 10

### Negation of the verb form sḏm.f

If an Egyptian wanted to say 'I do *not* hear' instead of 'I hear', he used what is called a *negative word*. The Egyptian language has many negative words; here we shall learn about two of them: ⌇⌇⌇ *n* and ⌇⌇⌇ *nn*, which can be used with the *sḏm.f* form of the verb.

The negative word is placed *before* the verb at the beginning of the sentence, and it changes the meaning of the verb in a rather strange way.

The *sḏm.f* form of the verb, as we have seen, can be used to indicate past, present and future tense. When it is used with the negative words ⌇⌇⌇ or ⌇⌇⌇ this is no longer the case:

1. ⌇⌇⌇ 𓀀𓁐𓏏 *n sḏm.f* has *past* meaning:

   e.g. ⌇⌇⌇ 𓂝𓐍𓏏𓊑 ⌇⌇⌇ 𓀀

   *n ir.i ḫt n ḥ3ty-ʿ* 'I did not do anything for the prince'.

2. ⌇⌇⌇ 𓀀𓁐𓏏 *nn sḏm.f* has *future* meaning:

   e.g. ⌇⌇⌇ 𓎟𓏤𓃀𓊽𓋔

   *nn wṯs.f dšrt* 'he shall not wear the Red Crown' *or* 'he shall never wear the Red Crown'.

In order to express the negative of the *present* tense, the element ⌇⌇⌇ *n* is placed *between* the verb-stem and the suffix-pronoun, where this pronoun is used; or *immediately after* the verb-stem when the suffix-pronoun is not used. The negative word ⌇⌇⌇ is then placed before the verb:

e.g. ⌇⌇⌇ 𓉐𓂋𓈖𓏏

   *n pr.n.f* 'he does not go out';

   ⌇⌇⌇ 𓀀𓁐𓂻𓊪𓀀𓏏

H

*n sḏm.n.i͗ ḫrw.f* 'I do not hear his voice';

*n sḏm.n nṯr ḫrw.f* 'the god does not hear his voice.'

## Sentences without verbs

There is no verb 'to be' in Egyptian. If an Egyptian wished to say 'the sun is in the sky', he would simply write ⟨hieroglyphs⟩ *r' m pt*, which translates as 'sun in sky'; we have to supply both the definite articles and 'is'.

The word order in sentences without verbs is the same as that in sentences with verbs; but since there is no object either in this kind of sentence, the order is:

1. subject  2. adverb or adverbial phrase.

e.g. 1. ⟨hieroglyph⟩  2. ⟨hieroglyph⟩

    1. *s*      2. *m niw̓t*

    1. man    2. in town

    (i.e. the man is in the town);

*or*

1. ⟨hieroglyph⟩  2. ⟨hieroglyph⟩

    1. *dpt*      2. *ḥr mw*

    1. boat    2. on water

    (i.e. the boat is on the water);

*or*

1. ⟨hieroglyph⟩  2. ⟨hieroglyph⟩

*ḥmt*      2. *'3*

    1. servant  2. here

    (i.e. the servant is here).

## ⟨hieroglyph⟩ *m* of predication

The Egyptians could not say 'the man is a scribe' but only 'the man is (as) a scribe'. The 'as' is expressed by the preposition ⟨hieroglyph⟩ *m*, which means 'in the position of', 'as'. Every sentence is made up of two parts: what is being spoken about (the subject) and what is being said about the subject (the predicate). Hence the term *m* of *predication*: the words introduced by this *m* describe the subject of the sentence.

e.g.  〔hieroglyphs〕 *s m sš* 'the man is a scribe'

〔hieroglyphs〕 *ḥmt m ḥmt* 'the woman is a servant'   *serving maid* 

*in positiong*

## Vocabulary to Lesson 10

〔hieroglyphs〕 *mhy* to be neglectful, to be forgetful, *ḥr* about

〔hieroglyphs〕 *bint* evil

〔hieroglyphs〕 *dwi* evilly

〔hieroglyphs〕 *nfrt* good

〔hieroglyphs〕 *k3* to raise

〔hieroglyphs〕 *r-pr* temple

〔hieroglyphs〕 *rmṯ* people

〔hieroglyphs〕 *'k* to enter

〔hieroglyphs〕 *wstn* to stride

〔hieroglyphs〕 *dw3* to adore

〔hieroglyphs〕 *sns* to worship

〔hieroglyphs〕 *sns* to worship

〔hieroglyphs〕 *wdḥw* altar

〔hieroglyphs〕 *i'ḥ* moon

〔hieroglyphs〕 *'3* here (adverb)

## EXERCISE 10

(a) *Write in hieroglyphs and transliteration*

1. I shall not be neglectful with regard to any counsel of my lord.
2. He does not speak (either) good (or) evil.
3. The man is in this city.
4. His daughter is in the house.
5. Behold, thou art my servant.

**(b) Translate into English**

1.

2.

3.

4.

5.

# LESSON 11

## Peculiarities of hieroglyphic writing

The reader will find in the Vocabularies a number of spellings which do not seem to conform to the rules of hieroglyphic writing so far learned. The following paragraphs will deal with six kinds of 'peculiar' writing.

## Abbreviations

Abbreviated writings are commonly used in monumental inscriptions, stereotyped phrases, titles, etc.

*e.g.*

*nsw* king

*nsw-bỉt* King of Upper and Lower Egypt (lit: he who belongs to the reed of Upper Egypt and the bee of Lower Egypt)

*nṯr nfr* the good god (epithet of king)

*k3 nḫt* strong bull (epithet of king)

*wḥm 'nḫ* repeating life (epithet of dead person)

*m3' ḫrw* justified (lit: true of voice, epithet applied to dead person, equivalent to our 'deceased')

*ḏd mdw* for recitation, to be recited

𓋹𓍑𓋴 *'nḫ wḏ3 snb* 'may he live, be prosperous, be healthy' (formula recited as mark of respect when king is mentioned)

𓄂 *ḥ3ty-'* local prince (lit: foremost in position)

𓊨,𓊨 *sp sn* twice, used:

  (a) to indicate that a sign or signs are repeated e.g. 𓏤𓀾𓂋𓏭𓂷 *sksk* 'to destroy'

  (b) to indicate repetition of a word to convey superlative—like 'very', 'much'

𓀾𓂋𓉐 *imy-r pr* steward (lit: overseer of the house)

## Sportive writings

𓄓 *imy-r* overseer (for 𓀾𓂋 *imy-r*); the hieroglyph 𓄓 depicts a tongue, i.e. 'what is in the mouth'; hence the meaning 'overseer' is a pun.

## Abbreviated writings

A few words almost never spell out the complete word:

𓂋𓏏𓀀𓀀𓀀 *rmṯ* men, people

𓎛𓈖𓏏 *ḥnḳt* beer

## Composite signs and monograms

1. Sometimes the ideogram is combined with a phonogram:

𓇍 *ii* come

𓇋𓊡 *is* go

𓄝𓏏 *ms* bring

𓈙𓅓 *šm* go

𓋴𓌂 *sšm* lead

𓏒 *in* bring

## 2. Some common monograms:

𓇳 *tr* season

𓆸 *rnp* be young

𓇔 *rs(w)* south

𓇗 *šm'w* Upper Egypt

𓇿 *ḫrt-hrw* daytime

𓊖 *ḫr(t)-nṯr* necropolis

𓉐 *'ḥ* palace

𓎛 *wḏ'* divide

## Graphic transposition

Sometimes signs are transposed, usually to give a more pleasing appearance:

𓅃𓏤 for 𓏤 𓅃 *tw*

為△ for △為 *t3*

↑為 for 為↑ *wd*

為 for 為 *wd3*

為△ for          *mr* 'pyramid'; this word is never written 為⊤◌△


## Honorific transpositions

With certain words, such as 'king' (⌇ *nsw*), 'god' (⌐ *ntr*), there is a tendency to write the word *before* closely connected words which are, in speech, pronounced first. This convention is observed in order to honour an important personnage. Abbreviated writings are frequent in such cases:

*ḥm-ntr* servant of god (priest)

*dw3-ntr* praise, thank

*ḥwt-ntr* temple (lit: mansion of god)

*sntr* incense

*s3 nsw* prince (lit: son of the king)

*pr nsw* palace (lit: house of the king)

*ḥtp dỉ nsw* an offering which the king gives

*mỉ R'* like Re

*mry ỉmn* beloved of Amun

*nsw* king, originally *nỉ-swt* 'he who belongs to the reed'.

## Hints on reading hieroglyphs

At all times, when reading hieroglyphs, it is as well to remember that the 'rules' were often broken. Lack of space sometimes forced a scribe to abbreviate his inscriptions by using fewer signs. Determinatives were often left out; plural signs and feminine endings were omitted. As we have seen above, spellings could vary.

At this stage, it is not necessary for the beginner to know why spellings varied. If he learns the hieroglyphic groups and their transliterations mechanically then he will not need to bother with theories about their etymology.

## Vocabulary to Lesson 11

*irt* 'performing' from verb *iri* 'to do'

*ḥtp* var. to be pleased, satisfied; to rest *ḥr* upon; to set (of sun)

*ḥtpw* gifts, offerings

*di* var. of *rdi* to give

var. of *nsw* king

*3pd* var. of goose, bird

*rnpt* growing thing, vegetable from *rnpi* to be young

*k3* var. of ox, bull

*mr.f* 'beloved of him' from var. *mri* to love

*m3' ḥrw* justified var. of *m3' ḥrw* true of voice

var. *šm'w* Upper Egypt

*šm'wt* Upper Egyptian

*itrt* row of shrines

*sntr* incense

*šs* alabaster

*ḥsb* to reckon

*t3 mḥw* Lower Egypt

*ḥnkt* offerings

*mrḥt* unguent

*mnḥt* clothing

*it* corn

**EXERCISE 11**

### (a)  Reading exercise 1

Study the following passage which is typical of inscriptions on Egyptian funerary stelae. The presentation of funerary offerings was called 🕭 ⸗ ⸗ △   *irt ḥtp-dỉ-nsw* 'performing (the rite called) "a boon-which-the-king-gives"'. From early on in Egyptian history, the phrase *ḥtp-dỉ-nsw* was used in reference to favours, such as gifts of clothing, food and drink, bestowed by a king upon his subjects. It seems that eventually all funerary gifts were considered to be gifts of the king to deities such as Osiris, the king of the dead, Anubis, the god of embalmment, or Geb, the earth-god; and that these deities passed on the gifts to the dead owner of the tomb in which the inscription is found.

e.g. Funerary wishes from the tomb of the Theban noble, Amenemhet (Dynasty XVIII):

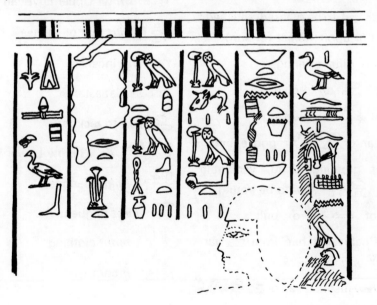

**Transcription, transliteration and translation:**

*htp-di-nsw*                 *Gb*       *psdt*

An offering which the king gives (to) Geb [and to the Ennead of the]

*itrt*      *mhwt*         *h3*          *m*     *t*      *h3*        *m*       *hnkt*

shrines of Lower Egypt: a thousand of bread, a thousand of beer,

*h3*        *m*      *k3w 3pdw*         *h3*        *m*        *hnkt nbt*

a thousand of oxen and geese, a thousand of every offering and

*rnpt*                  *sntr*     *nb*

growing thing and all (kinds of) incense, (that he may give it to)

*s3.f*        *mr.f*          *sš*         *imn-m-h3t*      *m3'-hrw*

his son, beloved of him, the scribe Amenemhat, [justified].

## (b) Reading exercise 2

Transcribe, transliterate and translate the following *htp-di-nsw* formula from the tomb of Amenemhet. Note that in this formula, the recipient is the son of Amenemhet, a scribe named Amenhotep:

*htp-di-nsw* formula for Amenhotep (restored somewhat)

## (c) Reading exercise 3

Study the following pictures which are of reliefs found in two New Kingdom tombs at Thebes (Luxor), Upper Egypt.

(i) Relief of Queen Nefertari, wife of Ramesses II of Dynasty XIX: transliterate and translate the hieroglyphs on the right-hand side of the picture:

(ii) *Left*:
Relief from the tomb of Nefertari:
transliterate and translate the
hieroglyphs at the top of the
relief:

(iii) *Below*:
Relief from the tomb of King
Horemheb, Dynasty XVIII:
transliterate and translate
the hieroglyphs in the picture (remember to read into
the faces of animals etc.):

## KEY TO EXERCISE 1

(3)

## KEY TO EXERCISE 2

(2)

## KEY TO EXERCISE 3

(a) 1.      2.      3.

    *'wy*          *mnty*          *spty*

4.      5.

    *rnpt 20*          *ḥf3w 75*

6.

    *dmỉ ḥ3*

(b)  1.  2 sides (*w3t 2*)
2.  365 gods (*365 n ntrw*)
3.  35 years (*rnpt 35*)
4.  ten thousand men (*s 10,000*)
5.  one hundred jugs of beer (*hnkt ds 100*)

## KEY TO EXERCISE 4

(a)  1.  *pr pn nfr*
2.  *nfrt tn*
3.  *hmt nt hm ntr*
4.  *pr nb*
5.  *imy-r mnh n niwt*

(b)  1.  an efficient overseer of fowlers (*imy-r shty mnh*)
2.  all good produce of the country (*inw nb(w) nfr(w) n sht*)
3.  every good thing (*ht nbt nfrt*)
4.  water for the father of the man (*mw n it s*)
5.  the handmaidens of the mistress of the house (*b3kwt nt hnwt nt pr*)

## KEY TO EXERCISE 5

(a)  1.  *r ky bw*
2.  *n Gb hn' R'*
3.  *m rn pn wr*
4.  *m t3w nbw*
5.  *m-b3h Pth*

(b) 1. night and day (*grḥ mỉ hrw*)
2. to the limits of the four supports of heaven (*r ḏrw sḫnwt nt pt*)
3. in the sanctuary of Ptah (*m ỉwnn n Ptḥ*)
4. on this beautiful day (*m hrw pn nfr*)


# KEY TO EXERCISE 6

1. *sḥtp-ỉb-Rˁ*
   (the heart of Re is satisfied)
   Sehetep-ib-Re

   *ỉmn-m-ḥ3t*
   (Amun is at the beginning)
   Ammenemes I (Dynasty XII)

2. *ḫpr-k3-Rˁ*
   (the spirit of Re comes into being)
   Kheper-ka-Re

   *s-n-Wsrt**
   (man of (the goddess) Wosret)
   Sesostris I (Dynasty XII)
   *this was formerly read *wsrtsn*
   (Usertsen), the version found in many
   of the early books on Egypt

3. *ḫˁ-k3w-Rˁ*
   (the spirits of Re appear)
   Kha-kau-Re

   *s-n-Wsrt*

   Sesostris III (Dynasty XII)

4. *n-m3ˁt-Rˁ*
   (belonging to the Truth of Re)
   Ne-maat-Re

   *ỉmn-m-ḥ3t*

   Amenemmes III (Dynasty XII)

5. *m3ˁt-k3-Rˁ*
   (Truth is the spirit of Re)
   Maat-ka-Re

   *ḥ3t-špswt*
   (foremost of noble women)
   Hatshepsut (Queen) (Dynasty XVIII)

6. *mn-ḫpr-R'*
   (the form of Re remains)
   Men-heper-Re

   *Ḏḥwty-ms*
   (born of Thoth)
   Tuthmosis III (Dynasty XVIII)

7. *nb-m3't-R'*
   (lord of the Truth of Re)
   Neb-maat-Re

   *ỉmn-ḥtp—ḥḳ3 w3st*
   (Amun is satisfied—ruler of Thebes)
   Amenophis III (Dynasty XVIII)

8. *nb-ḫprw-R'*
   (lord of the forms of Re)
   Neb-heperu-Re

   *twt-'nḥ-ỉmn*
   (living image of Amun)
   Tutankhamun (Dynasty XVIII)

9. *mn-m3't-R'*
   (the Truth of Re remains)
   Men-maat-Re

   *stḥ-y—mr-n-Ptḥ*
   (Seti beloved of Ptah)
   Sethos I (Dynasty XIX)

10. *wsr-m3't-R'-stp-n-R'*
    (powerful Truth of Re, chosen of Re)
    User-maat-Re-setep-en-Re

    *R'-msw—mry-ỉmn*
    (born of Re—beloved of Amun)
    Ramesses II (Dynasty XIX)

RM S SS

## KEY TO EXERCISE 7

(a) 1.  *pr . k pn nfr*

2.  *ḥmt . f nfrt*

3.  *m pr . f*

4.  *nỉwt . sn*

(b) 1. his little daughter (*s3t . f šrit*)

2. my wife, together with my daughter (*ḥmt . i ḥn' s3t . i*)

3. Lo, I am before you (*ist wi ḥft ḥr . k*)

4. Behold you are with me as my servant (*mk tw ḥn' . i m b3k . i*)

# KEY TO EXERCISE 8

(a) 1.    *ḏd . k rn . k n sš*

2.    *ḏd . k n s3 . k*

3.    *rš . f ḥr r . s*

4.    *h3b sš dpt tn*

5.    *ḥd . f r niwt s3t . f ḥn' . f*

(b) 1. Re crosses the sky in his barque (*ḏ3 R' pt m wi3 . f*)

2. The man goes down to the city upon another road (*h3 s r niwt ḥr kt w3t*)

3. The father sent his son to the city (*h3b it s3 . f r niwt*)

4. The sun appears upon the horizon and shines in the sky (*h' r' m 3ht wbn . f m pt*)

# KEY TO EXERCISE 9

(a) 1.    *rḫ sš sḥr m hrw pn*

2.    *h3b n . n nb . ṯn ht nbt nfrt*

3. gm.n sw ḥmt ḥr
   w3t

4. rdỉ.s n.f t ḥnḳt

5. ḏd.f n.n ỉb.f

(b) 1. I·gave bread to the hungry and beer to the thirsty (rdỉ.ỉt n ḥḳrw ḥnḳt n ỉbw)

2. Our good lord sends us a despatch about it (h3b n.n nb.n nfr š't ḥr.s)

3. After the servant had brought the donkey, he placed himself on its back (ỉn ḥm '3 dỉ.f sw ḥr s3.f)

# KEY TO EXERCISE 10

(a) 1. nn mḥy ḥr sḥr nb n
   nb.ỉ

2. n ḏd.n.f nfrt bint

3. s m nỉwt tn

4. s3t.f m pr

5. mk ṯw m b3k.ỉ

(b) 1. I did not raise my voice in the temple of my god (n ḳ3 ḥrw.ỉ m r-pr n nṯr.ỉ)

2. I do not do anything against any people evilly (n ỉr.n.ỉ ḥt nbt dwỉ r rmṯ nb)

3. He shall not receive bread (from) upon the altar of any god (nn šsp.f t ḥr wḏḥw n(y) nṯr nb)

4. The moon rejoices when the sun is in his horizon (ršỉ ỉ'ḥ r' m 3ḫt.f)

5. This beautiful woman is my sister; she does not speak any evil (nfrt tn m snt.ỉ n ḏd.n.s ḏwt nbt)

**KEY TO EXERCISE 11**

(c)　*Reading exercise 3*

     (i)　*Transliteration*: *m3' ḥrw ḥr wsîr ntr '3 nb îmntt*

         *Translation*:　　Justified before Osiris, the great god, lord of the West.

    (ii)　*Transliteration*: *ḏd mdw în 3st*

         *Translation*:　　For recitation by Isis.

                *ḥmt-nsw wrt nbt t3wy*

                The great royal wife (i.e. queen) mistress of the Two Lands

                *(nfrt-îry mrt n(t) mwt)|*

                (Nefertari beloved of Mut)|

                *m3' ḥrw ḥr wsîr ntr '3*

                justified before Osiris, the great god.

    (iii)　*Transliteration*: *ḏd mdw în 3st wrt*

         *Translation*:　　For recitation by Isis the great,

                *ḥnwt t3wy*

                mistress of the Two Lands.

                *wsîr nsw (ḏsr ḫprw r' stp n r')|*

                The Osiris, King (sacred form of Re, chosen of Re)|

                *s3 r' (ḥr m ḥb mry n îmn)|*

                the Son of Re (Horemheb beloved of Amun)|

                *m3' ḥrw ḥr (wsîr)*

                justified before (Osiris).

*Notes*

Osiris is the god of the dead who resides in the Underworld. 'The West' is a term used for the Underworld. Isis is the wife of Osiris. Mut is the wife of the god, Amun, of Thebes. Re is the sun god. Every dead person becomes 'an Osiris'; therefore, the reference to 'the Osiris' in example (iii) means that the king mentioned therein is dead.

# LIST OF HIEROGLYPHIC SIGNS

The following list contains most of the hieroglyphic signs used in this book, divided into groups. Within the groups, each sign is listed together with the name of the object it depicts, its uses and its transliteration/s (where applicable—some signs have no sound value but are found as determinatives (see further p. 66ff.) or ideographs only).

| Sign | Depicts | Meaning etc. |
|---|---|---|
| **Male figures** | | |
| | seated man | ideograph; determinative |
| | seated man and woman with plural strokes | det. |
| | man with hand to mouth | det. |
| | child seated with hand to mouth | det. |
| | bent man leaning on stick | ideo.; det. |
| | upright man with stick | ideo.; det. |
| | man with both arms raised | det. |
| | man striking with stick | det. |
| | seated god | det.; ideo. |
| | seated king | det.; ideo. |
| | noble seated on chair | det. |
| | mummy case | det. |
| | god with head of falcon with sun's disk on head | ideo. or det. for sun god e.g. Re |
| | god with head of ibis | ideo. or det. for god Thoth |

| Sign | Depicts | Meaning etc. |
|---|---|---|
| **Male figures** | | |
| | god with head of pig ( ? ) | ideo. for god Seth |
| | god with arms upraised | ideo. for god Ḥeḥ hence phonetically *ḥḥ* |
| **Female figures** | | |
| | seated woman | det. |
| | goddess with feather on head | ideo. or det. for Maat, goddess of truth |
| **Parts of the human body** | | |
| | head in profile | ideo.; det. |
| | face | ideo.; phon. *ḥr* |
| | eye | ideo.; phon. *ỉr* |
| | nose, eye and cheek | ideo.; det. |
| | mouth | ideo.; phon. r |
| | upper lip with teeth | ideo. |
| | arms outstretched | ideo.; phon. *k3* |
| | arms holding shield and axe | ideo. |
| | arms outstretched | ideo.; phon. *n* |
| | forearm | ideo.; phon. ' |
| | arm and hand holding loaf | det.; phon. *mỉ*; *m*; *d* |
| | hand | ideo.; det.; phon. *d* |
| | finger | ideo.; det.; phon. *ḏb'* |

| Sign | Depicts | Meaning etc. |
|---|---|---|
| | phallus | det.; phon.  $mt$; $\underline{h}mt$ |
| | legs walking | ideo.; det. |
| | legs walking backwards | det. |
| | leg | ideo.; det. |
| | foot | phon. $b$ |
| | foot surmounted by vase with water flowing from it | ideo. (purity) |

**Mammals**

| Sign | Depicts | Meaning etc. |
|---|---|---|
| | bull | ideo.; det. |
| | ass | det. |
| | kid | phon. $\dot{i}b$ |
| | recumbent lion | ideo.; phon. $rw$ |
| | desert hare | phon. $wn$ |

**Invertebrata**

| Sign | Depicts | Meaning etc. |
|---|---|---|
| | dung-beetle | ideo.; phon. $\underline{h}pr$ |
| | bee | ideo.; phon. $b\dot{i}t$ |

**Birds**

| Sign | Depicts | Meaning etc. |
|---|---|---|
| | Egyptian vulture | ideo.; phon. $3$ |
| | buzzard | phon. $t\dot{i}w$ |
| | vulture | phon. $mwt$ |
| | owl | phon. $m$ |
| | crested ibis | ideo.; phon. $3\underline{h}$ |
| | sacred ibis | det. Thoth |

| Sign | Depicts | Meaning etc. |
|---|---|---|
| *Birds* | | |
| | black ibis | phon. *gm* |
| | cormorant | phon. *'ḳ* |
| | swallow | phon. *wr* (N.B. swallow tail) |
| | sparrow | det. (N.B. rounded tail) |
| | goose | det.; phon. *gb* |
| | duck | det.; phon. *s3* |
| | duck flying | ideo.; phon. *p3* |
| | quail chick | phon. *w* |

*Signs grouped according to shape*

*Tall narrow signs*

| | | |
|---|---|---|
| | bundle of reeds | phon. *ỉs* |
| | bricklayer's tool? | phon. *ḳd* |
| | another form of sign above | |
| | butcher's knife | ideo.; phon. *nm* |
| | fire-drill | phon. *ḏ3* |
| | pestle | ideo.; phon. *tỉ* |
| | walking stick | ideo.; phon. *md* |
| | club | ideo.; phon. *ḥm* |
| | dagger | det. |
| | flowering reed | ideo.; phon. *ỉ* |
| | feather | ideo.; phon. *šw* |

| Sign | Depicts | Meaning etc. |
| --- | --- | --- |
| | bare palm-branch | det.; phon. *rnp* |
| | lotus | ideo.; phon. *ḫ3* |
| | folded cloth | phon. *s* |
| | pod | phon. *nḏm* |
| | feather on stand | ideo. (west) |
| | mast | phon. *'ḥ'* |
| | sceptre | ideo.; det.; phon. *w3s* |
| | sceptre | phon. *ḏ'm* |
| | sceptre | ideo. (Thebes) |
| | head and neck of canine | ideo.; phon. *wsr* |
| | crook | ideo.; det.; phon. *ḥḳ3* |
| | crook | phon. *'wt* |
| | throw-stick | det. |
| | pieces of wood tied together | ideo. (vigilant, etc.); phon. *rs* |
| | supporting pole | ideo.; det. |
| | post of balance | det. |
| | not known | phon. *nḏ* |
| | cloth on pole | ideo. (divinity); phon. *nṯr* |
| | mace | ideo.; phon. *ḥḏ* |
| | cord on stick | phon. *wḏ* or *wd* |
| | chisel | phon. *mr* |
| | sceptre | ideo.; det.; phon. *'b3* |

| Sign | Depicts | Meaning, etc. |
|---|---|---|
| **Tall narrow signs** | | |
| | heart and windpipe | phon. *nfr* |
| | lung and windpipe | phon. *sm3* |
| | milk jug in net | det.; phon. *mi* |
| | oar | det.; phon. *ḫrw* |
| | arrow-head | ideo.; phon. *sn* |
| | two crossed planks | ideo.; phon. *imi* |
| | loaf | ideo. (give) |
| | receptacle | det.; phon. *ḥn* |
| | three foxes' skins | phon. *ms* |
| | sandal-strap | ideo.; phon. *'nḫ* |
| | column | ideo.; phon. *ḏd* |
| | column | ideo.; phon. *iwn* |
| | palace | ideo. |
| | wick of twisted flax | phon. *ḥ* |
| | swab | det.; phon. *sk*; *w3ḫ* |
| | reed-floats | phon. *ḏb3* |
| | seat | ideo.; phon. *st* |
| | cow's skin pierced by arrow | det. |
| | scribe's outfit | ideo.; det. |
| | water-pot | ideo.; det.; phon. *ḥs* |
| | clump of papyrus | phon. *ḥ3* |

| Sign | Depicts | Meaning etc. |
| --- | --- | --- |
| | plant | ideo.; phon. *sw* |
| | two rushes | phon. *nn* |
| | bowl with legs | phon. *inỉ* |
| | chisel | det.; ideo.; *mnḫ* 'be efficient' |
| | lasso | phon. *w3* |
| | finger | ideo.; det.; phon. *ḏb'* |
| | arms holding shield and axe | ideo. |
| | sail | ideo.; det. |
| | papyrus roll | ideo.; phon. *mḏ3t* |
| | arms extended | ideo.; phon. *k3* |
| | leg and hoof of ox | ideo.; phon. *wḥm* |

**Low broad signs**

| Sign | Depicts | Meaning etc. |
| --- | --- | --- |
| | sky | ideo.; det.; phon. *ḥry* |
| | garden pool | ideo.; phon. *š* |
| | sandy tract | ideo.; phon. *ỉ* |
| | flat land with grains of sand | ideo.; det.; phon. *t* |
| | not known | phon. *m3'* |
| | not known | phon. *ỉm* |
| | netting needle filled with twine | ideo.; phon. *'ḏ* |
| | papyrus roll | ideo.; phon. *mḏ3t* |
| | loaf on reed mat | ideo.; phon. *ḥtp* |
| | crescent moon | ideo.; det. |

| Sign | Depicts | Meaning etc. |
|---|---|---|
| **Low broad signs** | | |
| | upper lip with teeth | ideo. |
| | tongue of ox ( ? ) | ideo.; phon. *ns* |
| | water skin | phon. *šd* |
| | sandy hill country | ideo.; det. |
| | whip | phon. *mḥ* |
| | whip | phon. *mḥ* |
| | bolt | ideo.; phon. *s* |
| | wooden column | phon. *'3* |
| | harpoon | ideo. |
| | adze | ideo.; phon. *nw* |
| | adze on block of wood | ideo.; det.; phon. *stp* |
| | tethering rope | phon. *t̲* |
| | elephant tusk | det.; phon. *bḥ*; *ḥ* |
| | finger | ideo.; det.; phon. *dk̲r* |
| | sledge | phon. *tm* |
| | road with shrubs | ideo.; det. |
| | door | ideo.; det.; phon. *'3* |
| | channel with water | ideo.; det.; phon. *mí* |
| | mouth | ideo.; phon. *r* |
| | basket | ideo.; phon. *nb* |
| | basket with handle | phon. *k* |

| Sign | Depicts | Meaning etc. |
| --- | --- | --- |
| | alabaster basin | det.; phon. $\d{h}b$ |
| | reed fence | phon. $\check{s}sp$ |
| | oxyrhynchus fish | ideo.; phon. $\underline{h}3$ |
| | ripple of water | phon. $n$ |
| | three ripples of water | ideo.; phon. $mw$ |
| | a fish | det.; phon. $\dot{i}n$ |
| | forepart of lion | ideo. |
| | goat skin | ideo.; phon. $\underline{h}n(w)$ |
| | draught-board | phon. $mn$ |
| | animal's belly | ideo.; phon. $\underline{h}$ |
| | house | ideo.; phon. $pr$ |
| | backbone | ideo.; phon. $3w$ |
| | sickle | ideo.; phon. $m3$ |
| | forearm with hand holding round loaf | phon. $m\dot{i}$; $m$ |
| | reeds | ideo.; det.; phon. $sm$ |
| | horns of ox | ideo.; phon. $wp$ |
| | hoe | det.; phon. $mr$ |
| | phallus | det.; phon. $mt$ |
| | branch | ideo.; det.; phon. $\d{h}t$ |
| | sky with star hanging beneath | det. |
| | herb | det.; phon. $\d{h}n$; $\dot{i}s$ |

| Sign | Depicts | Meaning etc. |
|---|---|---|
| *Low broad signs* | | |
| | bow-string | ideo.; det.; phon. *rwd* |
| | pool with lotuses | ideo.; phon. *š3* |
| | sun rising over hill | ideo. |
| | sandy hill | ideo.; phon. *dw* |
| | band of string or linen | det.; phon. *'rḳ* |
| | back of something | ideo.; phon. *s3* |
| | horned viper | ideo.; phon. *f* |
| | cobra | phon. *d* |
| | forearm | ideo.; phon. *'* |
| *Low narrow signs* | | |
| | stool | phon. *p* |
| | stone slab | det. |
| | tongue of land | det. |
| | irrigation canal | det. |
| | sandy hill-slope | phon. *ḳ* |
| | loaf | det. |
| | bread | ideo.; phon. *t* |
| | hill over which sun is rising | ideo.; phon. *ḫ'* |
| | back of something | ideo.; phon. *s3* |
| | piece of crocodile skin | phon. *km* |

| Sign | Depicts | Meaning etc. |
|---|---|---|
| | bowl with smoke of incense rising from it | ideo.; det. |
| | basket of fruit or grain | det. |
| | bundle of flax tied at top | det.; phon. *dr* |
| | potter's kiln | ideo.; phon. *t3* |
| | jar-stand | ideo.; det.; phon. *g* |
| | butcher's block | phon. *ḥr* |
| | well full of water | det.; phon. *ḥm*; *bỉ3* |
| | well full of water | det.; phon. *ḥm*; *bỉ3* |
| | heart | ideo. |
| | cord | ideo.; phon. *šs* |
| | loop of cord | phon. *šn* |
| | hobble for cattle | phon. *md* |
| | ear of ox? | ideo.; det.; phon. *ỉdn* |
| | sun | ideo.; det. |
| | moon with lower half obscured | ideo.; det.; phon. *psd* |
| | placenta? | phon. *ḫ* |
| | threshing floor covered with grain | det.; phon. *sp* |
| | village with cross-roads | ideo.; det. |
| | cartouche in original round form rather than the later ⬭ | det. |

| Sign | Depicts | Meaning etc. |
|---|---|---|
| *Low narrow signs* | | |
| 𓇶 | sunshine | det.; ideo.; phon. *wbn* |
| 𓆸 | flower? | phon. *wn* |
| 𓍱 | coil of rope | det.; phon. *šn* |
| ⌐ | doubtful | phon. *gs* |
| ✶ | star | ideo.; det.; phon. *sb3*; *dw3* |
| ▽ | bowl | phon. *nw* |
| 𓏊 | beer-jug | ideo.; det. |
| 𓆏 | frog | det |
| 𓆤 | tadpole | phon. *ḥfn* |
| 𓉐 | reed shelter | ideo..; phon *h* |

# EGYPTIAN-ENGLISH VOCABULARY

**3**

𓄿𓅱𓏏 *3wt* gifts

𓄿𓊪𓂧 *3pd* goose, bird

𓄿𓊪𓂧 *3pd* goose, bird

𓄿𓏏 *3ḫt* horizon

𓊨𓏏 *3st* Isis

**ỉ**

𓇋𓄿𓎛 *ỉ'ḥ* moon

𓇋𓃹𓈖𓈖 *ỉwnn* sanctuary

𓄣 *ỉb* heart

𓇋𓃀𓏏 *ỉbt* thirst

𓇋𓃀𓅯 *ỉbỉ* to be thirsty

� *ỉmy-r* overseer

𓇋𓏠𓈖 *ỉmy-r* overseer

𓇋𓏠𓈖 *ỉmn* Amun (god)

𓋀 *ỉmnt* the West *ỉmntt*

𓇋𓈖 *ỉn* by

𓏏 *ỉnỉ* to bring

𓏏 *ỉnw* produce

𓁹 *ỉrỉ* to do, act, make

K

𓁹 *ỉrt* eye

𓇋𓏏 *ỉt* corn

𓇋𓏏 *ỉt* father

𓇋𓏏𓏤 *ỉtrt* row of shrines

**'**

𓂝𓄿 *'3* donkey

𓂝𓄿 *'3* great

𓂝𓄿 *'3* here

𓋹𓏤 *'nḫ* to live

𓂝𓎡 *'ḳ* to enter

**w**

𓅱𓄿𓊨𓏏 *w3st* Thebes

𓅱𓄿𓏏 *w3t* road, path, way

𓃭𓄿 *wỉ3* sacred barque

𓃭𓈖 *wbn* to rise

𓃭𓈖 *wbn* to shine

𓅨𓂋 *wr* great

𓅨𓂋 *wr* prince, noble

𓁹𓀭 *wsỉr* Osiris

𓅱𓊃𓂋 *wsr* powerful

*Wsrt* Wosret (goddess)

*wstn* to stride

*wts* to wear, carry lift, up

*wdḥw* altar

**b**

*b3kt* handmaiden

*bînt* evil

*bw* place

**p**

*pr* house

*prî* to go out

*psḏt* Ennead

*pt* sky

*Ptḥ* Ptah (god)

**m**

*m* in, from, with

*m* on, in

*m33* to see

*m3ˀ ḫrw* justified

*M3ˀt* Maat, goddess of Truth

*m3ˀt* truth

*m3ˀ ḫrw* justified

*mîˀ* like

*mw* water

*mwt* Mut

*mn* to remain

*mnḫ* to be efficient

*mnḫt* clothing

*mnt* thigh

*mrî* to love

*mry* beloved

*mrḥt* unguent

*mhy* to neglect, forget

*mḥ* cubit

*m-ḫ3t* in front of

*m-ḫt* after

*ms* born

**n**

*n* to, of

*nb* any, every, all

*nb* lord, master

*nfr* good, beautiful, happy

*nfrt* good

*nḥḥ* eternity

*nsw* king (of Upper Egypt)

*nsw-bît* king (of Upper and Lower Egypt)

*nṯr* god

**r**

*r* mouth

*r* to, against

*r* utterance

*Rꜥ* Re (sun god)

*Rꜥ* Re

*Rꜥ* Re

*rꜥ* sun

*rꜥ* sun

*r-pr* temple

*rmt* people

*rn* name

*rnpt* vegetable

*rnpt* year

*rḫ* to know

*ršw* to rejoice

*rdỉ* to give, place

*r-ḏrw* to the limits

**h**

*hꜣỉ* to go down

*hꜣb* to send

*hrw* day, daytime

**ḥ**

*ḥꜣt* front, forehead

*ḥꜣty-ꜥ* local prince

*ḥfꜣw* snake

*ḥm* Majesty

*ḥm(t)* servant

*ḥm-nṯr* priest

*ḥmt* woman, wife

*ḥnꜥ* with

*ḥnwt* mistress

*ḥnwt* mistress

*ḥnkt* offerings

*ḥnkt* beer

*ḥr* face, upon

*ḥs* to freeze

*ḥsỉ* to turn back

*ḥsb* to reckon

*ḥkꜣ* ruler

*ḥkr* hungry man

*ḥtpw* gifts, offerings

*ḥḏt* White Crown (of Upper Egypt)

*ḫ*

ḫꜥỉ to appear, shine

ḫꜥỉ to appear

ḫpr to become

ḫprw form

ḫft in front of, before

ḫr before

ḫrw voice, cry

ḫt thing

ḫdỉ to fare downstream

*ẖ*

ẖt belly, body

*s*

s man

s3 back

s3 son

s3t daughter

sb3 door

sbw food

spt lip

sns to worship

snt sister

snṯr incense

sḥtp to pacify ꜥ

sḥtp to satisfy

sḫnt four supports of heaven

sḫr plan, counsel

sḫt country

sḫty fowler, peasant

sš scribe

st woman

stỉ Seti (king)

stp choice

sḏm to hear, obey

š't despatch

špsỉ to be noble

šmꜥw Upper Egypt

šrr small

šs alabaster

šsp to accept, receive

šsp daylight

šsp palm (unit of length)

šsp statue

*k*

k3 to raise

**k**

𓏲𓃾 *k3* ox, bull

𓃒 *k3* ox, bull

𓂓𓏤 *k3* spirit

𓎡𓏭 *ky* other, another m.

𓆎𓏏𓊖 *kmt* the Black Land (Egypt)

𓎡𓏏 *kt* another, other f.

**g**

𓅬𓃀𓅆 *Gb* Geb (god)

𓅠𓅓𓏏 *gmỉ* to find

𓎼𓂋𓎛 *grḥ* night

**t**

𓏏𓏤 *t* bread

𓇾𓏤 *t3* earth

𓇿𓏤𓏤 *t3wy* the Two Lands (Egypt)

𓇾𓏤𓎔𓅱 *t3 mḥw* Lower Egypt

𓏏𓅱𓏏 *twt* image, statue

**d**

𓇼𓀢 *dw3* to adore

𓇼𓇳 *dw3t* Underworld

𓂧𓊪𓏏 *dpt* boat

𓂧𓏠𓅉 *dmỉ* town

𓂧𓂋𓏏 *drt* hand

𓂧𓊚 *ds* jug

𓂧𓏤𓏏 *dšrt* Red Crown (of Lower Egypt)

𓂧𓈅 *dšrt* red land (desert)

**ḏ**

𓆓𓏏𓀁 *ḏ3ỉ* to cross

𓈋 *ḏw* mountain

𓈋𓂧𓏺 *ḏwỉ* evilly

𓈋𓂧𓏏 *ḏwt* evil, sadness

𓁟𓏏𓅆 *Ḏḥwty* Thoth (god)

𓆓𓋴𓂋 *ḏsr* sacred

𓆓𓏏 *ḏt* eternity

𓆓𓂧 *ḏd* to say, tell *n* to someone

𓌃𓏤 *ḏd mdw* 'for recitation'

# ENGLISH-EGYPTIAN VOCABULARY

**A**

accept

act

adore

against

alabaster

all

altar

Amun

another

any

appear

**B**

back

beautiful

beer

before

belly

bird

Black Land (Egypt)

boat

body

born

bread

bring

bull

by

**C**

carry

choose

city

clothing

corn

counsel

country

cross

cubit

**D**

daughter

day

| | |
|---|---|
| daylight | forget |
| daytime | 'for recitation' |
| desert | freeze |
| despatch | from |
| do | front |
| donkey | **G** |
| door | Geb |
| **E** | gifts , |
| earth | give , , |
| efficient | god |
| Egypt | go down |
| Ennead | go out |
| enter | good , |
| eternity , , | goose , |
| every | great |
| evil , | **H** |
| evilly | hand , |
| eye | handmaiden |
| **F** | happy |
| face | hear |
| father | heart |
| find | here |
| food | horizon |

house

hungry man

I

image

in

incense

J

jug

K

king

know

L

lift up

like

lip

live

lord

love

Lower Egypt

M

majesty

make

man

mistress

moon

mountain

mouth

N

name

night

O

obey

of

offerings

other

overseer

ox

P

pacify

palm

peasant

people

place

plan

powerful

priest

| | | |
|---|---|---|
| prince | shrines | |
| produce | sister | |
| **R** | sky | |
| raise | small | |
| Re | snake | |
| receive | son | |
| recitation   see 'for recitation' | statue | |
| reckon | stride | |
| Red Crown | sun | |
| rejoice | supports (four) of heaven | |
| rise | **T** | |
| road | tell | |
| ruler | temple | |
| **S** | Thebes | |
| sail downstream | thigh | |
| sanctuary | thing | |
| satisfy | thirst | |
| say | thirsty | |
| scribe | this | |
| see | Thoth | |
| send | to | |
| servant | town | |
| shine | turn back | |

Two Lands (Egypt)

U
Underworld
unguent
upon
Upper Egypt
utterance

V
vegetable
voice

W
water
wear
West
White Crown
wife
with ,
woman ,
worship ,

Y
year

## FURTHER READING

ANDREWS, C., *The Rosetta Stone,* British Museum Publications, London, 1981.

ERMAN, A., *The ancient Egyptians: a sourcebook of their writings,* Harper Torchbooks, New York, 1966.

FAULKNER, R.O., *A concise dictionary of Middle Egyptian*, Oxford University Press, Oxford, 1962.

GARDINER, A.H., *Egyptian grammar: being an introduction to the study of hieroglyphs,* 3rd ed. (rev.), Oxford University Press, Oxford, 1957.

GARDINER, A.H., "The Egyptian origin of the Semitic alphabet", in *The Journal of Egyptian Archaeology*, 3, 1916, pp.1-16.

HOOKER, J.T., *ed., Reading the past: ancient writing from cuneiform to the alphabet,* British Museum Publications, 1990.

LICHTHEIM, M., *Ancient Egyptian literature,* 3 vols, University of California Press, Berkeley,1973-80.

MILLARD, A.R., "The infancy of the alphabet", in *World Archaeology*, 17, no.3, 1986, pp.390-98.

RAY, J.D., "The emergence of writing in Egypt", in *World Archaeology*, 17, no.3, 1986, pp.307-16.

SHENNUM, D., *English-Egyptian index of Faulkner's Concise dictionary of Middle Egyptian,* Undena Publications, Malibu, 1977.

WILLIAMS, R.J., "Scribal training in ancient Egypt", in *Journal of the American Oriental Society*, 92, 1972, pp.214-21.

# GENERAL INDEX

Narmer: slate palette of, 35
    unification of Egypt, 1
Napoleon Bonaparte, Expedition to Egypt, 4 foll.
Nefertiti, 51
negation, 105
negative words, 105
Nelson, Admiral Lord Horatio, 5
Nile, Battle of, 5
non-verbal sentences, 106
nouns, 74
numbers, 77, 78

obelisk, derivation of word, 52
obelisks, taken from Philae to Dorset for W. J. Bankes, 16
'Oedipus Aegyptiacus', 12
Old Egyptian, 47
Old Persian, 33
Osiris, 114

Pachom, St, 49
palette of Narmer, 35
palettes, slate, 35
paper, 42
papyrus, 42, 43
'Pekinese dogs', 6
Pharaoh, the term, 51
Philae: obelisks, 16
    temple of Isis, 39
Phoenician alphabet, 28
phonetic complements, 66
phonograms, 25 foll., 65
pictographs, 22 foll.
picture writing, 24
plural, 75
prepositions, 84, 85
pronouns: 91
    *see also under* dependent pronouns:
    suffix-pronouns
pronunciation of Egyptian, 58
proto-Semitic alphabet, 28
Ptolemaic script, 47
Ptolemaios, 15, 16, 18
Ptolemy V, Epiphanes, 8

Pyramid Texts, 47
Pyramids: Battle of, 5
    derivation of word, 52

Rameses, 20
Ramesses, 20
reading hieroglyphic writing, 113
rebus, 25, 36
Redouté, P., 5
Roman alphabet, 26
Rosellini, 21
Rosetta Stone, 8, 15, 17
Rougé, J. de, 21
Russian: alphabet (Cyrillic), 26, 27
    language, 44

Sacy, S. de, 9
Sahidic, dialect in Coptic, 50
Saint-Hilaire, G., 4, 6
Sanskrit: alphabet, 27
    language, 44
Sargon the Great, 30
Savigny, M-J. de, 5, 6
schoolboys, exercise letters, 41
scribes, 39 foll.
*sḏm.f* verb form: negation, 105
    paradigm, 97
Semitic, 44
sense signs, 23
Serâbit el-Khâdim, 28
Sethe, K., 21
Shem, son of Noah, 44
Shenute, 49
singular, 75
sound signs, 25
Sphinx (Giza), 53
sphinxes, 53
sportive writings, 110
Strabo, 11
Sub-Akhmimic, dialect in Coptic, 50
suffix-pronouns, 92
Sumer, 30
Sumerians, 29

tablets, clay, 30